Exploring
Thessalonians

A DEVOTIONAL COMMENTARY

GEORGE R. KNIGHT

REVIEW AND HERALD® PUBLISHING ASSOCIATION
Since 1861 | www.reviewandherald.com

The author assumes full responsibility for the accuracy of all facts and quotations as cited in this book.

All Bible texts quoted are the author's unless otherwise noted.

Texts credited to Message are from *The Message.* Copyright © 1993, 1994, 1995, 1996, 2000, 2001, 2002. Used by permission of NavPress Publishing Group.

Bible texts credited to Moffatt are from: *The Bible: A New Translation,* by James Moffatt. Copyright by James Moffatt 1954. Used by permission of Harper & Row Publishers, Incorporated.

Scripture quotations marked NASB are from the *New American Standard Bible,* copyright © 1960, 1962, 1963, 1968, 1971, 1972, 1973, 1975, 1977, 1995 by The Lockman Foundation. Used by permission.

Texts credited to NEB are from *The New English Bible.* © The Delegates of the Oxford University Press and the Syndics of the Cambridge University Press 1961, 1970. Reprinted by permission.

Texts credited to NIV are from the *Holy Bible, New International Version.* Copyright © 1973, 1978, 1984, International Bible Society. Used by permission of Zondervan Bible Publishers.

Texts credited to New Jerusalem are from *The New Jerusalem Bible,* copyright © 1985 by Darton, Longman & Todd., Ltd., and Doubleday & Co., Inc. Reprinted by permission of the publisher.

Texts credited to NKJV are from the New King James Version. Copyright © 1979, 1980, 1982 by Thomas Nelson, Inc. Used by permission. All rights reserved.

Bible texts credited to NRSV are from the New Revised Standard Version of the Bible, copyright © 1989 by the Division of Christian Education of the National Council of the Churches of Christ in the U.S.A. Used by permission.

Bible texts credited to Phillips are from J. B. Phillips: *The New Testament in Modern English,* Revised Edition. © J. B. Phillips 1958, 1960, 1972. Used by permission of Macmillan Publishing Co.

Texts credited to REB are from *The Revised English Bible.* Copyright © Oxford University Press and Cambridge University Press, 1989. Reprinted by permission.

Bible texts credited to RSV are from the Revised Standard Version of the Bible, copyright © 1946, 1952, 1971, by the Division of Christian Education of the National Council of the Churches of Christ in the U.S.A. Used by permission.

Verses marked TLB are taken from *The Living Bible,* copyright © 1971 by Tyndale House Publishers, Wheaton, Ill. Used by permission.

This book was
Edited by Gerald Wheeler
Cover designed by Left Coast Design
Cover illustration by Jerry Blank
Typeset: 11/14 Bembo

PRINTED IN U.S.A.

16   15   14   13   12   5   4   3   2   1

Library of Congress Cataloging-in-Publication Data
Knight, George R.
  Exploring Thessalonians : a devotional commentary.
      p. cm.
  1. Bible. N.T. Thessalonians—Commentaries. I. Title.
  BS2725.53.K55 2012
  227'.81077—dc23

                              2011038287

ISBN 978-0-8280-2643-7

Dedicated to

Robert and Sarah Fusté,
beloved children with
whom I share the journey
toward God's kingdom

Other books by George R. Knight (selected):

A Brief History of Seventh-day Adventists
A Search for Identity: The Development of Seventh-day Adventist Beliefs
A User-friendly Guide to the 1888 Message
Ellen White's World
I Used to Be Perfect (Andrews University Press)
If I Were the Devil
Joseph Bates: The Real Founder of Seventh-day Adventism
Lest We Forget
Meeting Ellen White
Myths in Adventism
Organizing for Mission and Growth: The Development of Adventist
    Church Structure
Reading Ellen White
Sin and Salvation
The Apocalyptic Vision and the Neutering of Adventism
The Cross of Christ
Walking With Ellen White
William Miller and the Rise of Adventism (Pacific Press)

The Exploring Series
Exploring Ecclesiastes & Song of Solomon
Exploring Mark
Exploring Galatians & Ephesians
Exploring Hebrews
Exploring the Letters of John & Jude
Exploring Romans

A study guide to *Exploring Thessalonians* is available on adventistbook
    center.com.

Forthcoming Exploring volumes
Exploring James

To order, call 1-800-765-6955.

Visit us at www.reviewandherald.com for information on other
Review and Herald® products.

Contents

Book I: Exploring 1 Thessalonians

Introduction to the First Letter to the Thessalonians

Book II: Exploring 2 Thessalonians

Introduction to the Second Letter to the Thessalonians

Occasion and Purpose of 2 Thessalonians
Major Themes in 2 Thessalonians
Structure and Outline of 2 Thessalonians
2 Thessalonians' Relevance for the Twenty-first Century

Exploring the "Exploring" Idea

Exploring Thessalonians is the seventh volume in a series of user-friendly commentaries aimed at helping people understand the Bible better. While the books have the needs and abilities of laypeople in mind, they will also prove beneficial to pastors and other church leaders. Beyond individual readers, the "Exploring" format will be helpful for church study groups and in enriching participation in midweek meetings.

Each volume is best thought of as a devotional commentary. While the treatment of each passage seeks to develop its exegetical meaning, it does not stop there but moves on to practical application in the daily life of believers in the twenty-first century.

Rather than focusing on the details of each verse, the "Exploring" volumes seek to give readers an understanding of the themes and patterns of each biblical book as a whole and how each passage fits into its context. As a result, they do not attempt to solve all of the problems or answer all the questions related to a given portion of Scripture.

In an effort to be user-friendly these devotional commentaries on the Old and New Testaments present the entire text of each biblical book treated. The volumes divide the text into "bite-sized" portions that are included immediately before the comments on the passage. Thus readers do not have to flip back and forth between their Bibles and the commentary.

The commentary sections aim at being long enough to significantly treat a topic, but short enough for individual, family, or group readings.

The translation of each New Testament book is my own, and claims no special merit. Although I have based it on the original languages, in making it I have conferred with several English versions. While not being a "technical achievement," the translation has sought to take every significant translational problem and issue into consideration and to remain as close as possible to the original text of the Bible. In order to accomplish that goal the translation employs word-for-word translation wherever possible but utilizes thought-for-thought translation when word-for-word fails adequately to carry God's message from the original languages and cultures into modern English.

George R. Knight
Rogue River, Oregon

Foreword

Paul's two letters to the Christians in Thessalonica stand close to the heart of all who have an interest in the second coming of Jesus and the events that will take place in relation to that climactic event in world history. The letters provide us with the apostle Paul's fullest description of the Second Advent and the great apostasy that will precede it. In the process they supply us with details found nowhere else in Scripture. On the other hand, what they do teach on the topic integrates smoothly with snapshots of Christ's coming in the four Gospels and 1 Corinthians 15:51–57 and the broader treatment found in the book of Revelation and the prophetic themes presented in Daniel's writings.

Beyond eschatology, other highlights in the Thessalonian epistles feature the importance of the apostolic word to the church, the functional equality of the members of the divine Trinity, a pastoral model of ministry, the need for progressive sanctification, and the careful balance revealed in Paul's approach to redemptive church discipline. In short, the two letters to Thessalonica provide a fruitful field of biblical investigation. As such, they deserve extended and thoughtful study.

One can read this devotional commentary as a freestanding book or in conjunction with the online study guide developed to accompany it. The study guide to *Exploring Thessalonians* will provide those who use it with an opportunity to let the biblical books speak to them personally through structured questions before they turn to the commentary itself. (To download and print the free study guide, go to www.AdventistBookCenter.com, find the book *Exploring Thessalonians*, then "Click for Details" and follow the instructions for downloading the guide.)

I would like to express my appreciation to my wife, who typed my handwritten manuscript; and Gerald Wheeler and JoAlyce Waugh, who shepherded the manuscript through the publication process.

I trust that *Exploring Thessalonians* will be a blessing to each of its readers as they seek to learn more of their Lord and as they put that knowledge into practice in daily living.

Exploring

First
Thessalonians

Introduction to the
First Letter to the Thessalonians

First Thessalonians has the distinction of being the earliest extant written document in Christian history with the possible exception of Galatians. Thus it provides "an excellent example of apostolic teaching during the first generation of the Christian Church, less than twenty-five years after the beginning of Jesus' ministry" (Bromiley, *International,* vol. 4, p. 834). As such, "it offers the earliest direct insight into the early Christian mission and the life of an early, fundamentally non-Jewish-Christian church. It also contains the oldest summary of Paul's missionary proclamation to a non-Jewish community" (Freedman, vol. 6, p. 516). Because of its many "firstnesses," 1 Thessalonians deserves to be read with special care.

One thing that stands out in this short letter is its practical nature. While the authors of all of the New Testament letters wrote them to meet current issues in the various Christian communities, some of them, such as Romans, Hebrews, and Galatians, are heavy on theological content. By way of contrast, 1 Thessalonians emphasizes pastoral concern to an uncommon extent. Thus Abraham Malherbe points out that "First Thessalonians reflects . . . pastoral care of a fledgling church more clearly than any of Paul's other letters" (Malherbe, *Paul,* p. 2). In the process, the apostle puts himself forth as both a motherly "nurse taking care of her children" (1 Thess. 2:7, RSV) and a "father" exhorting and encouraging them (verse 11).

A careful reader will notice several things about the Thessalonian correspondence. One is that "neither letter contains even one explicit citation from the OT" (Beale and Carson, p. 871). Also missing are references to the great personalities of the Old Testament, such as Abraham, Moses, or David; any of its cultic institutions, such as the Temple or priesthood; or any of its great events, such as the Exodus or Exile. We can explain the absence of such material by the fact that Paul was writing primarily to a Gentile congregation not familiar with the Hebrew Bible.

More surprising perhaps is the lack of many Christian and even Pauline ideas. Thus we find no mention of justification, baptism, the Lord's Supper, the church as the body of Christ, or the contrast between law and grace. In fact, the concept of saving grace, one of Paul's favorite convictions, is totally missing in 1 Thessalonians, and he mentions it only twice in the second letter (2 Thess. 1:12; 2:16). The absence of those key New Testament concepts, of course, is due to the circumstances of the Thessalonian believers and the apostle's purpose in writing.

The Place of Thessalonica in the Empire

In order most fully to understand the Thessalonian correspondence, it is important to have a basic grasp of the geographic, economic, religious, and political situation of the Roman city of Thessalonica in the middle of the first century of the Christian era. The first thing to note is the city's strategic location in the Roman Empire. Thessalonica was not only the largest and most prosperous city in northern Greece, but it had a first-class harbor that placed it in the north/south travel and trade axis from the Mediterranean to the hinterlands of Macedonia. Beyond that, it was located about midway on the Via Egnatia, the main land road from the Adriatic Sea to Byzantium (Istanbul) with its access to the Roman province of Asia (modern Turkey), which positioned it on the east/west axis of trade and travel. Beyond location, the natural resources of the surrounding territory also furthered the city's prosperity.

The strategic location of Thessalonica was not lost on either Rome or Paul and his missionary colleagues. Both would utilize the city as a center for their efforts in the area. In 146 B.C. the Empire made the city the capital of Macedonia. And in 42 B.C. Thessalonica became a "free city" because of its support of the emperor. Free-city status normally brought with it exemption from taxation, the privilege of not having Roman troops stationed within the city walls, and governance according to traditional custom rather than being obligated to submit to the Roman form of civic government (see Green, pp. 8-20).

Thus being a free city was not a privilege to take lightly or squander. Yet it is that very status that Paul and his fellow missionaries challenged, as emphasized in Acts 17 when Jason and some of the other converts were "dragged . . . before the city authorities" with the charge of having turned "the world upside down" and "acting against the decrees of Caesar, saying that there is another king, Jesus" (verses 6, 7, RSV).

To complicate matters even further, the Empire combined religion and politics, the union between the two climaxing in emperor worship. That worship "was a political and diplomatic act that was intimately intertwined with the economic realities [and favors] of the relationship between Thessalonica and Rome" (Green, p. 41). The Thessalonian converts, of course, not only adopted a new religion, but, more seriously, they turned "from idols to serve a living and true God" (1 Thess. 1:9). In doing so they threatened the favored economic and political situation of the city and brought persecution upon themselves (see Pfeffer, p. 11).

Before moving on to the founding of the Christian church in Thessalonica, we should note that the pagan religion of the city not only had ties to emperor worship but also to sexual licentiousness through the worship of such false deities as Aphrodite, the goddess of love. It is in that context that Paul makes his strong call for sexual purity among the new believers in 1 Thessalonians 4:3-8.

Bringing the Gospel to Thessalonica

Acts 16:9 represents a major turning point in Paul's ministry. In a night vision at Troas he saw a man begging him, saying, "Come over to Macedonia and help us" (RSV). With that vision the focal point of Paul's mission shifted from Asia Minor to southeastern Europe, especially Macedonia and Greece.

With Silas, Timothy, and Luke, the apostle crossed the Aegean Sea and began preaching in Philippi, where they not only founded a church but where Paul and Silas received a severe beating and imprisonment (Acts 16:11-40).

Their next stop was 90 miles away in Thessalonica, the site of a Jewish

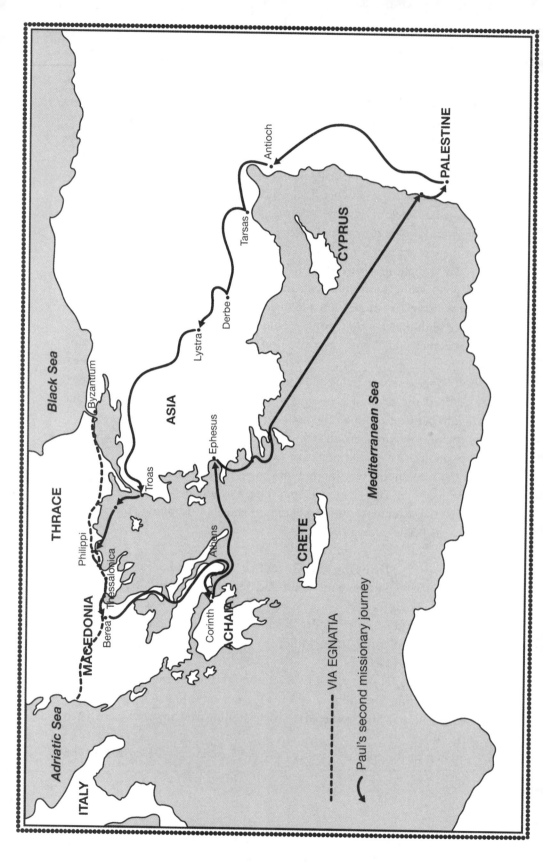

synagogue. There, according to his usual practice, the apostle preached first to the Jews for three Sabbaths, arguing "with them from the scriptures, explaining and proving that it was necessary for the Christ to suffer and to rise from the dead, and saying, 'This Jesus, whom I proclaim to you, is the Christ'" (Acts 17:1-3, RSV).

The good news of the Thessalonian mission is that a fair number of converts joined the church. Acts 17:4 lists three subsets of new members: (1) some of the Jews, (2) a "great many" of the Greeks who worshipped at the synagogue, and (3) quite a few of the prominent women.

The bad news of the mission to Thessalonica was that the evangelistic success brought a vigorous reaction from the Jews, who were "jealous," gathered a crowd of rabble, and began to cause trouble (verse 5). Here we need to pause and point out that they had good reason for their reaction. The Thessalonian synagogue had for some time been working among the Gentile population with good results. Not only had they convinced many of the town's upper class women and/or the "wives of the leading men" (Marshall, *Acts*, p. 277), but also a "great multitude" (*plēthos polu*) of the Greek men who had been attending the Jewish services but had not converted to Judaism because of the circumcision requirement. Here was a truly successful synagogue. They had for years been proselyting among Thessalonica's large Gentile population, when suddenly Paul and his associates arrived in town and destroyed the hard work of a decade or more. No wonder they were "jealous."

Their hostility soon led to action. The Jewish leaders couldn't find Paul and his colleagues, so they hauled Jason and some of the other converts to the city authorities, "crying, 'These men who have turned the world upside down have come here also, and Jason has received them; and they are all acting against the decrees of Caesar, saying that there is another king, Jesus.'" They eventually let Jason and the other converts loose, but the new believers had to send Paul and Silas away (Acts 17:5-10, RSV).

Acts 17:1-10 tells us a great deal about why Paul wrote what he did in his first letter, why he had to leave there so abruptly (1 Thess. 2:17), why the Thessalonian church underwent persecution (2:14), and why, perhaps, some had even been martyred for the newfound faith (4:13-18).

There is one question, however, that we must ask of the Acts 17 passage: Did Paul's evangelistic team really found the Thessalonian church in just three weeks? That appears to be an extremely short period to establish such a stable and faithful congregation.

With that in mind, a number of scholars have suggested that a considerable time lapse may have occurred between the time Paul finished preaching in the synagogue in Acts 17:4 and when the Jews initiated the persecution of verse 5. Thus Leon Morris points out that "there is nothing in the narrative to exclude a further period among the Gentiles" (Morris, *The Epistle*, p. 17). And arguing from the biblical evidence, William Ramsay asserts that "Paul clearly refers to a long and very successful work in Thessalonica." He suggests a period of about six months (Ramsay, p. 228).

Two pieces of evidence especially point to a longer ministry in Thessalonica. The first is Paul's claim in 1 Thessalonians 2:9 that they had worked "night and day" so that they might not be a burden to the church while they preached the gospel to them. Coupled with that statement is one in Philippians 4:16 in which Paul writes that "even in Thessalonica you sent me help once and again" (RSV).

While those comments imply a longer period than three weeks, the balancing evidence in the epistle indicating the suddenness of Paul's separation from the congregation and the incompleteness of his instruction to them suggests a relatively short ministry in that important city.

Writing the First Letter to the Thessalonians

While we do not know the exact length of time Paul stayed in Thessalonica, we do know that his next stop was Berea, about 45 miles to the west (Acts 17:10). Perhaps he went no farther in the hope that he might soon return to Thessalonica. But such was not to be, because "Satan hindered us" in spite of the strong desire to return (1 Thess. 2:18).

Berea supplied a happy respite for Paul and his fellow evangelists. After having been driven out of Philippi and Thessalonica, they were welcomed by the Jewish community in Berea, who "received the word with all eagerness, examining the scriptures daily" to verify the gospel message (Acts 17:11, RSV). The result was a large group of converts. But the calm working conditions soon evaporated when the Thessalonian Jews heard of the success in Berea and sent representatives who began "stirring up and inciting the crowds" (verse 13). So once again Paul found himself bundled up and sent off, this time by sea to distant Athens. Silas and Timothy remained in Berea for a time, but Paul soon requested their presence in the new mission field of southern Greece (verses 14, 15).

Their departure left the new Thessalonian believers isolated, with the nearest Christian congregations being in Philippi 90 miles or four days travel to the east and Berea 45 miles or a two-day journey to the west. The Thessalonians were not only alone, but their isolation took place in the midst of a very aggressive Jewish community that had incited the Gentile population against them. At best it was a tense and dangerous situation. No one wanted the power of Rome to descend on the city to threaten or remove its political autonomy and privileged economic status because of some group causing disturbances by proclaiming another king than Caesar (verse 7).

The result was persecution of the new and inadequately indoctrinated congregation in Thessalonica. "In a situation like that," David Jackman writes, "wouldn't it be the easiest thing in the world for these young Christians to say, 'Well, let's call this whole thing off! Let's just admit that we have been temporarily hoodwinked by a very clever operator, a travelling salesman for religion, who actually took us in. Now let's just drift quietly back to the synagogue. OK, let's apologize, let's eat humble pie for a few weeks, and then forget the whole episode ever happened at all'?" (Jackman, p. 17).

By the time Paul reached Athens he had begun to fear that possibility. And his psychological situation wasn't getting any better. After all, even though the Athenians didn't run him out of their pagan metropolis with its philosophical sophistication, they did largely ignore him in spite of some creative preaching (verses 16-34).

Paul's next stop was Corinth, in which he remained 18 months. The Corinthian ministry enabled the apostle to catch his breath, even though it was not a trouble-free location. He needed the rest. After his harrowing experiences in Macedonia and being ignored in Athens, he was at a low point. Reflecting upon his previous difficulties, he wrote to the Corinthians that when he came to them "I was feeling far from strong; I was nervous and rather shaky" (1 Cor. 2:3, Phillips). Leon Morris observes that "a very human Paul was clearly a very discouraged man at this point in his career" (Morris, *Themes*, p. 3).

It was during this period that he wrote his first letter to the Thessalonians, who were also in difficult circumstances. His concern for them had actually become acute during his stay in Athens. By that time Timothy and Silas had joined him after completing the grounding of the Berean church in the faith.

That had been good for that congregation, but the insufficiently instructed Thessalonian church increasingly caused Paul anxiety. He desperately wanted to visit them personally but found himself repeatedly blocked by "Satan" (1 Thess. 2:18). In his subsequent distress he wrote that "when we could bear it no longer, we were willing to be left behind at Athens alone, and we sent Timothy, our brother and God's servant in the gospel of Christ, to establish you in your faith and to exhort you, that no one be moved by these afflictions" (1 Thess. 3:1-3, RSV). Again he states that "when I could bear it no longer, I sent that I might know your faith, for fear that somehow the tempter had tempted you and that our labor would be in vain" (verse 5, RSV).

It was Timothy's return to Paul, who was by that time in Corinth (Acts 18:5), that prompted the apostle to write 1 Thessalonians. He was overjoyed that they remained in the faith and had not rejected Paul or his ministry to them (1 Thess. 3:6) and that "our visit to you was not in vain" (1 Thess. 2:1, RSV). Their faithfulness comforted and brought joy to the discouraged apostle (verses 7-9).

Nevertheless, he realized that the congregation still had problems and that they needed counsel and hope. The counsel included an exhortation to sexual purity (4:1-8), to love one another (4:9, 10), to continue to work in spite of their belief in the nearness of the Second Advent (4:11, 12; 5:14), to respect the leaders of their congregation (5:12, 13), to not be vengeful to those who had injured them (5:15), to rejoice and give thanks in spite of their situation (5:16, 18), to pray constantly (5:17), and not to reject those claiming the prophetic gift, but rather to test them (5:19-21). Each of those counsels, of course, was extremely appropriate for the situation in which the Thessalonian believers found themselves.

The same can be said for the hope of the Second Advent and the resurrection of believers discussed in 1 Thessalonians 4:13-5:10. Some had apparently become discouraged over the deaths of fellow believers. That worry led Paul to one of his truly great passages on the Second Advent and the resurrection hope, one bracketed with the words "hope," "comfort," and "encourage" (4:13, 18; 5:11). Meanwhile, the Thessalonians were not to let the seeming delay of Christ's coming discourage them (5:1, 2).

We can determine the date of Paul's letters to the Thessalonians with a fair degree of accuracy. Acts 18:12 indicates that most of his 18 months in Corinth (verse 11) took place before Gallio became proconsul. Secular history indicates that Gallio's administration began in the summer of A.D. 51. Thus Paul likely arrived in Corinth early in A.D. 50 and left in the late summer or autumn of A.D. 51. As a result, he wrote both of the Thessalonian letters in A.D. 50-51, which puts them less than 20 years after Christ's crucifixion.

Regarding the authorship of the Thessalonian letters, both of them note that they are from Paul, Silvanus (the Latin form of Silas), and Timothy (1 Thess. 1:1; 2 Thess. 1:1). That does not necessarily mean that all three shared in composing them, even though the vast majority of first person pronouns are "we" rather than "I." Some see that usage as a "courteous gesture" that Timothy and Silas, as cofounders of the congregation, "were in agreement with what Paul wrote" (Stott, p. 25). The fact that it is Paul who commands that the first letter be read publicly in the congregation (1 Thess. 5:27) and that he adds his customary signature at the end of 2 Thessalonians (3:17; cf. 1 Cor. 16:21; Col. 4:18; Philemon 19) supports such a conclusion. There are, as we might expect, other places in both letters that reflect Paul's individuality as author (1 Thess. 2:18; 3:5; 2 Thess. 2:5). Those first person singular references, though in the minority, stand at significant junctures in the letter when Paul allows his personal concern for the Thessalonians to show forth, thereby indicating his authorship.

The Sequence of the Thessalonian Correspondence

A final issue dealing with the letters to Thessalonica is their sequence. Whereas some students of the topic have reversed the order and placed 2 Thessalonians first, there is no compelling evidence for doing so. Donald Gutherie sums up the situation nicely when he writes that "none of these reasons is convincing taken separately, nor is the cumulative effect any more so" (Gutherie, p. 601; for the evidence itself, see pp. 599-601 and Jewett, pp. 21-30).

The fact that each of the problems addressed in 1 Thessalonians (including persecution, the Advent, and idleness) seems to have deepened in 2 Thessalonians supports the traditional order of compostition. Beyond that, 2 Thessalonians 2:15 seemingly refers to a prior letter. More conclusive are the extensive personal reminiscences in 1 Thessalonians 2:17–3:6, which are absent from the other letter. Such a situation would be quite natural if the traditional sequence is maintained, but unnatural if reversed. George Milligan finds that argument so convincing that he claims that the reversal "is excluded by I [Thess.] ii.17–iii.6 which could hardly have been written by St. Paul, if he had previously addressed a letter to Thessalonica" (Milligan, p. xxxix).

Major Themes of 1 Thessalonians

While it is true that "the Thessalonian epistles are the least dogmatic [systematically doctrinal] of all the Pauline epistles" (Tenney, vol. 5, p. 725), several theological themes do stand out in 1 Thessalonians.

1. *God as sovereign.* "God the Father" finds a significant place in the greetings of both of the Thessalonian letters (1 Thess. 1:1; 2 Thess. 1:2). In the face of the pagan deities worshipped in Thessalonica, the God that Paul preaches is the "living and true God" (1 Thess. 1:9) who is the source of the Christian gospel (2:2). God is not only living, but He is loving (1:4), a providential guide in human lives (3:11), and peaceful (1:1). In addition, He is the one who calls individuals into the Christian faith (1:4) and continues to summon them into "His own kingdom and glory" (2:12). And, finally, God will be faithful in bringing to completion the work that He has begun (5:24). In the meantime, He hears the prayers of His followers (5:17), sanctifies them (5:23), and gives them the Holy Spirit (4:8). In short, God stands at the very center of 1 Thessalonians. He is sovereign in their history, conversion, and final redemption.

2. *Jesus is "Lord."* Right from the first verse in both 1 and 2 Thessalonians we find a high view of Jesus. Whereas Jesus is His human name, in each epistle His divine nature flashes through in the phrase "the Lord Jesus Christ." "Lord," is a title rather than a name. For Jewish readers it represented divinity. After all, the Septuagint (the Greek translation of the Old Testament) uses the word to render "Yahweh," the very name of God. Gentile readers would have picked up the same message, since the pagan world often employed that term to refer to their deity. When Paul

used it he was putting Jesus in the highest place.

The word "Christ" also expresses Jesus' divinity, being the Greek translation of "Messiah," which means "anointed one." While one could regard a king or a priest as anointed, the Jews expected that in due course God would send *the* anointed one, someone who would do His will in a special way. One expectation of that hope would be that the Christ would rescue God's people from their Roman oppressors. Thus Paul's calling Jesus the Messiah would have aroused heightened ideas of His mission among those familiar with the Hebrew Bible.

Paul's linking of "God the Father" with "the Lord Jesus Christ" in the first verse of each of the Thessalonian letters is a definite signal of Jesus' divinity and His equality with the Father. Morris puts it succinctly when he writes that "it is not easy to see how any created being, anyone less than God, could be linked with God the Father in such a way" (Morris, *Themes*, p. 31).

3. *The Second Advent.* The major theological contribution of 1 Thessalonians lies in the realm of eschatology or the doctrine of the end of history when Christ returns. First Thessalonians 4:13-5:11 is Paul's most extensive treatment of the topic in any of his letters. Only 1 Corinthians 15:51-57 compares with it. Together they present Paul's general understanding of the topic.

The eschatological passage in 1 Thessalonians addresses two issues particularly troubling the Thessalonian believers. Chapter 4:13-18 answers the question of "What happens to Christians who die before the Lord comes?" while 1 Thessalonians 5:1-11 deals with "When will the Lord come?" In answering the first question, the apostle provides us with many details found nowhere else in the New Testament. Then, in addressing the second, he shifts the focus from knowing the exact time to being ready for the event, in much the same way that Jesus did in Matthew 24, 25. The second letter will considerably elaborate upon both questions.

4. *Holy living.* Often connected with the Second Advent, generally as a motivator, is the topic of sanctification or holy living. That is particularly evident in the transition between the two major sections of 1 Thessalonians. Verse 13 of chapter 3 closes off the personal part of the letter with a prayer that God would establish the believers in holiness so that they might be prepared for the "coming of our Lord Jesus, with all His

holy ones." Then follows two chapters of counsel on holy living interspersed and intertwined with doctrinal teaching on the Second Advent. It climaxes with 1 Thessalonians 5:23, in which Paul writes, "May the God of peace Himself sanctify you entirely, and may your spirit and soul and body be preserved complete and blameless at the coming of our Lord Jesus Christ."

5. *Positive encouragement as a model for ministry.* While Paul urged higher standards in the Thessalonian church, he mixed that call constantly with the ministry of encouragement. That model provides the church and its members with an often overlooked aspect of its communal life. All too often, people such as Paul who have high standards and who desire to see them manifested in others come across as negative and critical. While Christians must confront sin, their concern for others must always be positive and supportive and rooted in love.

The apostle begins his ministry of encouragement in his letter's second verse. In fact, verses 2-10 are one massive paragraph of encouragement and positive reinforcement. That trend resurfaces in a major way in 1 Thessalonians 3:6-10. Even though the church was far from perfect and even though he had some strong exhortations for them on how to conduct their lives, the apostle operated with the awareness of the fact that "when we know we are loved, we are able to receive from people things that would otherwise be hard to hear and might produce great resistance" (Jackman, p. 111).

Structure and Outline of 1 Thessalonians

Some of the New Testament letters are difficult to outline, but that is not true of 1 Thessalonians. It is quite straightforward with an introduction (1:1), a body divided into two parts (personal matters in 1:2-3:13 and exhortation and instruction in 4:1-5:22), and a conclusion (5:23-28). The following outline represents that structure:

    I. Greeting (1:1)
    II. Personal matters (1:2-3:13)
        A. Thanksgiving for the Thessalonians (1:2-10)
        B. Paul's work among them (2:1-12)
        C. Their reception of the gospel (2:13-16)

1 Thessalonians' Relevance for the Twenty-first Century

For a world in which death is an ongoing reality, the book of 1 Thessalonians is as relevant as relevant can be. The promises of the resurrection and of the translation of all God's people at Christ's second coming provide words of comfort in a world short on hope in the face of death. The force of the explicit teachings on Christian hope in 1 Thessalonians 4:13-18 will continue until the end of time to be an encouragement to Christians facing death and those in bereavement.

Also pertinent for those looking for the return of Jesus is Paul's refocusing of the center of the topic away from the time of the event and toward being ready when it does take place (1 Thess. 5:1-11). Too many Christians get all excited about time, but have little interest, let alone practice, in being ready for the Advent by living the life of God's love in their family, workplace, and neighborhood.

Of additional significance for the church in a hostile world is the promise that God will bring to completion that which He has begun in both the church and in individual Christian lives (5:23, 24). We serve a God who will not forsake us no matter how bad it gets or how much opposition we face around us. Closely related to that pledge of God's faithfulness until the end are the promises of assurance in 1 Thessalonians related to tests in our personal lives and in His continuing guidance of the church. One of the messages of the letter is that Christians can be confident that they are on the right track if they test their lives against the original apostolic teachings (4:2). When they wonder if their Christianity is genuine, the letter responds that if they have a faith that works, a love that labors, and a hope that perseveres (1:3) in the context of a walk with God (4:1), they are Christians indeed. They are to examine everything by the apostolic teaching delivered to them in the founding of the church. Even that which purports to be future prophetic guidance of the church needs to be judged by that standard (5:19-21).

Along that line is the relevance of the call for sexual morality in 1 Thessalonians 4:1-8. The church lived within a Greek culture that saw nothing wrong with sexual exploration and experimentation. We exist in the same kind of "Greek" culture today as postmodernism tells us that there are no universal rights and wrongs in our private sexual lives, as long as such acts take place between consenting adults.

Lastly, 1 Thessalonians speaks to the twenty-first-century church because of its insights into the dynamics of a local congregation and the role of true pastoral ministry. Both church leaders and members can learn much of contemporary value from this early (probably earliest) Christian letter.

List of Works Cited in 1 and 2 Thessalonians

Althaus, Paul. *The Theology of Martin Luther.* Philadelphia: Fortress, 1966.

Ante-Nicene Fathers, 10 vols. Ed. Alexander Roberts et al. Peabody, Mass.: Hendrickson, 1994.

Apostolic Fathers. Trans. J. B. Lightfoot and J. R. Harmer. Ed. Michael W. Holmes. 2nd ed. Grand Rapids: Baker, 1989.

Bainton, Roland H. *Here I Stand: A Life of Martin Luther.* New York: New American Library, 1950.

Barclay, William. *The Letters to the Philippians, Colossians, and Thessalonians.* 2nd ed. The Daily Study Bible. Edinburgh: Saint Andrew Press, 1960.

Barnes, Albert. *Notes on the New Testament.* Grand Rapids: Baker, 2009, vol. 12, part 2, pp. 9-102.

Bauer, Walter. *A Greek-English Lexicon of the New Testament and Other Early Christian Literature.* 3rd ed. Rev. and ed. by Frederick Danker. Chicago: University of Chicago, 2000.

Beale, G. K. *1-2 Thessalonians.* The IVP New Testament Commentary Series. Downers Grove, Ill.: InterVarsity, 2003.

———. *The Use of Daniel in Jewish Apocalyptic Literature and in the Revelation of St. John.* Eugene, Oreg.: Wipf and Stock, 2010.

Beale, G. K., and D. A. Carson, eds. *Commentary on the New Testament Use of the Old*

Testament. Grand Rapids: Baker Academic, 2007.

Berkouwer, G. C. *Man: The Image of God*. Grand Rapids: Eerdmans, 1962.

Best, Ernest. *A Commentary on the First and Second Epistles to the Thessalonians*. Harper's New Testament Commentaries. Peabody, Mass.: Hendrickson, 1986.

Bicknell, E. J. *The First and Second Epistles to the Thessalonians*. Westminster Commentaries. London: Methuen, 1932.

Bonhoeffer, Dietrich. *The Cost of Discipleship*. Rev. ed. New York: Collier, 1959.

Bromiley, Geoffrey W., ed. *The International Standard Bible Encyclopedia*. Rev. ed., 4 vols. Grand Rapids: Eerdmans, 1979-1988.

―――――., ed. *Theological Dictionary of the New Testament*, abridged ed. Grand Rapids: Eerdmans, 1985.

Bruce, F. F. *1 and 2 Thessalonians*. Word Biblical Commentary. Nashville: Thomas Nelson, 1982.

Calvin, John. "Commentary on the First Epistle to the Thessalonians." "Commentary on the Second Epistle to the Thessalonians." *Calvin's Commentaries*. Grand Rapids: Baker, 1999, vol. 21, pp. 233-362.

―――――. *Institutes of the Christian Religion*, 2 vols. Ed. John T. McNeill. Philadelphia: Westminster, 1960.

Clarke, Adam. "The Second Epistle of Paul the Apostle to the Thessalonians." In *The New Testament of Our Lord and Saviour Jesus Christ*. New ed. New York: Abingdon, n.d., vol. 2, pp. 562-577.

Clarke, James W. "The First and Second Epistles to the Thessalonians: Exposition." In *The Interpreter's Bible*. Nashville: Abingdon, 1955, vol. 11, pp. 243-339.

Cullman, Oscar. "Immortality of the Soul or Resurrection of the Dead?" In Krister Stendahl, *Immortality and Resurrection*. New York: Macmillan, 1965, pp. 9-53.

Demarest, Gary W. *1, 2 Thessalonians, 1, 2 Timothy, Titus*. The Communicator's Commentary. Waco, Tex.: Word, 1984.

Denney, James. *The Epistles to the Thessalonians*. The Expositor's Bible. New York: A. C. Armstrong and Son, 1903.

Ellicott, Charles John. *Commentary on the Epistles of St. Paul to the Thessalonians*. Classic Commentary Library. Grand Rapids: Zondervan, 1957.

Ellingworth, Paul, and Eugene A. Nida. *A Translator's Handbook on Paul's Letters to the Thessalonians*. London: United Bible Societies, 1976.

Evans, Craig A., and Stanley E. Porter, eds. *Dictionary of New Testament Background*. Downers Grove, Ill.: InterVarsity, 2000.

Fee, Gordon D. *The First and Second Letters to the Thessalonians*. The New International Commentary on the New Testament. Grand Rapids: Eerdmans, 2009.

―――――. *The First Epistle to the Corinthians*. The New International Commentary on the New Testament. Grand Rapids: Eerdmans, 1987.

Findlay, George G. *The Epistles to the Thessalonians*. The Cambridge Bible. Cambridge University, 1904.

Frame, James Everett. *Epistles of St. Paul to the Thessalonians*. International Critical

Commentary. Edinburgh: T&T Clarke, n.d.

Freedman, David Noel, ed. *The Anchor Bible Dictionary*, 6 vols. New York: Doubleday, 1992.

Froom, Le Roy Edwin. *The Prophetic Faith of Our Fathers: The Historical Development of Prophetic Interpretation*, 4 vols. Washington, D.C.: Review and Herald, 1946-1954.

Furnish, Victor Paul. *1 Thessalonians, 2 Thessalonians*. Abingdon New Testament Commentaries. Nashville: Abingdon, 2007.

Gaventa, Beverly Roberts. *First and Second Thessalonians*. Interpretation: A Bible Commentary for Teaching and Preaching. Louisville: John Knox, 1998.

Gillespie, Thomas W. *The First Theologians: A Study in Early Christian Prophecy*. Grand Rapids: Eerdmans, 1994.

Gorday, Peter, ed. *Colossians, 1-2 Thessalonians, 1-2 Timothy, Titus, Philemon*. Ancient Christian Commentary on Scripture. Downers Grove, Ill.: InterVarsity, 2000.

Green, Gene L. *The Letters to the Thessalonians*. The Pillar New Testament Commentary. Grand Rapids: Eerdmans, 2002.

Guthrie, Donald. *New Testament Introduction*. 4th ed. Downers Grove, Ill.: InterVarsity, 1990.

Harrison, Everett F., and Donald A. Hagner. "Romans." In *The Expositor's Bible Commentary*. Rev. ed. Grand Rapids: Zondervan, 2008, vol. 11, pp. 19-237.

Hawthorne, Gerald F., Ralph P. Martin, and Daniel G. Reid, eds. *Dictionary of Paul and His Letters*. Downers Grove, Ill.: InterVarsity, 1993.

Henry, Matthew. "The Second Epistle of St. Paul to the Thessalonians." In *Matthew Henry's Commentary*. Peabody, Mass.: Hendrickson, 1991, vol. 6, pp. 638-649.

Heschel, Abraham Joshua. *God in Search of Man: A Philosophy of Judaism*. New York: Farrar, Straus and Giroux, 1955.

Hiebert, D. Edmond. *The Thessalonian Epistles: A Call to Readiness*. Chicago: Moody, 1971.

Holmes, Michael W. *1 and 2 Thessalonians*. The NIV Application Commentary. Grand Rapids: Zondervan, 1998.

Horn, Siegfried H. et al. *Seventh-day Adventist Bible Dictionary*. Washington, D.C.: Review and Herald, 1960.

Hubbard, Moyer V. *Christianity in the Greco-Roman World*. Peabody, Mass.: Hendrickson, 2010.

Jackman, David. *The Authentic Church*. Fearn, Great Britain: Christian Focus, 1998.

Jaeger, Werner. "The Greek Ideas of Immortality." In Krister Stendahl, *Immortality and Resurrection*. New York: Macmillan, 1965, pp. 97-114.

Jamieson, Robert, A. R. Fausset, and David Brown. "The Second Epistle of Paul the Apostle to the Thessalonians." In *A Commentary on the Old and New Testaments*. Peabody, Mass.: Hendrickson, 2008, vol. 3, part 3, pp. 471-479.

Jewett, Robert. *The Thessalonian Correspondence: Pauline Rhetoric and Millenarian Piety*. Philadelphia: Fortress, 1986.

Josephus, Flavius. *Josephus: Complete Works*. William Whiston, ed. Grand Rapids: Kregal, 1960.

Kittel, Gerhard, and Gerhard Friedrich, eds. *Theological Dictionary of the New Testament*, 10 vols. Grand Rapids: Eerdmans, 1964-1976.

Knight, George R. *The Cross of Christ: God's Work for Us*. Hagerstown, Md.: Review and Herald, 2008.

————. *Exploring Ecclesiastes and Song of Solomon*. Hagerstown, Md.: Review and Herald, 2006.

————. *Exploring the Letters of John and Jude*. Hagerstown, Md.: Review and Herald, 2009.

Ladd, George Eldon. *The Blessed Hope*. Grand Rapids: Eerdmans, 1956.

LaRondelle, Hans K. "The Historicist Method in Adventist Interpretation." In *Spes Christiana*, vol. 21 (2010), pp. 79-89.

————. *How to Understand the End-time Prophecies of the Bible: The Biblical-contextual Approach*. Sarasota, Fla.: First Impressions, 1997.

————. *Light for the Last Days: Jesus' End-time Prophecies Made Plain in the Book of Revelation*. Nampa, Idaho: Pacific Press, 1999.

Lightfoot, J. B. *Notes on Epistles of St. Paul*. J. R. Harmer, ed. Thornapple Commentaries. Grand Rapids: Baker, 1980.

Malherbe, Abraham J. *Paul and the Thessalonians: The Philosophic Tradition of Pastoral Care*. Philadelphia: Fortress, 1987.

————. *The Letters to the Thessalonians*. The Anchor Bible. New York: Doubleday, 2000.

Malina, Bruce J. *The New Testament World: Insights From Cultural Anthropology*. 3rd ed. Louisville: Westminster John Knox, 2001.

Marshall, I. Howard. *1 and 2 Thessalonians*. New Century Bible Commentary. Grand Rapids: Eerdmans, 1983.

————. *The Acts of the Apostles*. The Tyndale New Testament Commentaries. Grand Rapids: Eerdmans, 1980.

Meeks, Wayne A. *The First Urban Christians: The Social World of the Apostle Paul*. New Haven, Conn.: Yale University, 1983.

Milligan, George. *St. Paul's Epistles to the Thessalonians*. Grand Rapids: Eerdmans, 1952.

Moffatt, James. "The First and Second Epistles to the Thessalonians." In *The Expositor's Greek Testament*. Grand Rapids: Eerdmans, 1988, vol. 4, pp. 1-54.

Morris, Leon. *1, 2 Thessalonians*. Word Biblical Themes. Dallas: Word, 1989.

————. *The Epistles of Paul to the Thessalonians*. Tyndale New Testament Commentaries. Grand Rapids: Eerdmans, 1957.

————. *The First and Second Epistles to the Thessalonians*. Rev. ed. The New International Commentary on the New Testament. Grand Rapids: Eerdmans, 1991.

————. *The First and Second Epistles to the Thessalonians*. The New International Commentary on the New Testament. Grand Rapids: Eerdmans, 1959.

Moulton, James Hope, and George Milligan. *The Vocabulary of the Greek Testament*. Grand Rapids: Eerdmans, 1930.

Mounce, William D. *Mounce's Complete Expository Dictionary of Old and New Testament Words*. Grand Rapids: Zondervan, 2006.

Neil, William. *The Epistle of Paul to the Thessalonians*. Moffatt New Testament

Commentary. London: Hodder and Stoughton, 1950.

———. *St. Paul's Epistles to the Thessalonians*. Torch Bible Commentaries. London: SCM, 1957.

Nicene and Post-Nicene Fathers, First Series, 14 vols. Ed. Philip Schaff. Peabody, Mass.: Hendrickson, 1994.

Nichol, Francis D., ed. "The Second Epistle of Paul the Apostle to the Thessalonians." In *The Seventh-day Adventist Bible Commentary*. Washington, D.C., 1953-1957, vol. 7, pp. 259-282.

Pfeffer, Leo. *Church, State, and Freedom*. Rev. ed. Boston: Beacon, 1967.

Ramsay, W. M. *St. Paul the Traveller and the Roman Citizen*. Grand Rapids: Baker, 1962.

Richards, E. Randolph. *Paul and First-Century Letter Writing: Secretaries, Composition and Collection*. Downers Grove, Ill.: InterVarsity, 2004.

Richardson, Allan. *An Introduction to the Theology of the New Testament*. New York: Harper and Row, 1958.

Ridderbos, Herman. *Paul: An Outline of His Theology*. Grand Rapids: Eerdmans, 1975.

Robertson, Archibald Thomas. *Word Pictures in the New Testament*, 5 vols. Grand Rapids: Baker, 1931.

Rogers, Cleon L., Jr., and Cleon L. Rogers III. *The New Linguistic and Exegetical Key to the Greek New Testament*. Grand Rapids: Zondervan, 1998.

Ryken, Leland, James C. Wilhoit, and Tremper Longman III, eds. *Dictionary of Biblical Imagery*. Downers Grove, Ill.: InterVarsity, 1998.

Schaff, Philip, ed. *The Creeds of Christendom*. 6th ed., 3 vols. Rev. by David S. Schaff. Grand Rapids: Baker, 1985.

Shea, William H. *Daniel 7-12: Prophecies of the End Time*. Boise, Idaho: Pacific Press, 1996.

Stedman, Ray C. *Waiting for the Second Coming: Studies in Thessalonians*. Grand Rapids: Discovery House, 1990.

Stendahl, Krister. *Immortality and Resurrection*. New York: Macmillan, 1965.

Stern, David H. *Jewish New Testament Commentary*. Clarksville, Md.: Jewish New Testament Publications, 1992.

Stott, John R. W. *The Message of Thessalonians: The Gospel and the End of Time*. The Bible Speaks Today. Downers Grove, Ill.: InterVarsity, 1991.

Stowers, Stanley K. *Letter Writing in Greco-Roman Antiquity*. Philadelphia: Westminster, 1986.

Tenney, Merrill C., ed. *The Zondervan Pictoral Encyclopedia of the Bible*, 5 vols. Grand Rapids: Zondervan, 1975, 1976.

Thayer, Joseph H. *Thayer's Greek-English Lexicon of the New Testament*. Peabody, Mass.: Hendrickson, n.d.

Thomas, Robert L. "1 Thessalonians," "2 Thessalonians." In *The Expositor's Bible Commentary*, rev. ed. Grand Rapids: Zondervan, 2006, vol. 12, pp. 361-485.

Walker, L. W. *What About the New Theology?* Edinburgh: T and T Clarke, 1907.

Wanamaker, Charles A. *The Epistles to the Thessalonians*. The New International Greek Testament Commentary. Grand Rapids: Eerdmans, 1990.

Weima, Jeffrey A. D. "1 Thessalonians," "2 Thessalonians." *Zondervan Illustrated Bible Backgrounds Commentary*. Grand Rapids: Zondervan, 2002, vol. 3, pp. 404-443.

White, Ellen G. *Education*. Mountain View, Calif.: Pacific Press, 1952.

———. *The Great Controversy Between Christ and Satan*. Mountain View, Calif.: Pacific Press, 1950.

Whiteley, D. E. H. *Thessalonians*. The New Clarendon Bible. London: Oxford University, 1969.

Witherington, Ben, III. *1 and 2 Thessalonians: A Socio-Rhetorical Commentary*. Grand Rapids: Eerdmans, 2006.

Wright, N. T. *Paul for Everyone: Galatians and Thessalonians*. Louisville: Westminster John Knox, 2004.

Part I

Introductory Matters

1 Thessalonians 1:1

1. A Weighty Introduction

1 Thessalonians 1:1
> *¹Paul and Silvanus and Timothy,*
> *To the church of the Thessalonians in God the Father and the Lord*
> *Jesus Christ:*
> *Grace to you and peace.*

That verse may look simple enough, but it is packed with meaning. But before we get to the theological issues imbedded in the text we need to look at the author of the letter—or is it authors, since it mentions Silvanus and Timothy along with Paul? In answering that question a glimpse of the identity of the three men will be helpful.

Silvanus is the Latin form of Silas, whom we first meet in Acts 15 as a bearer of the letter of the Jerusalem Council to Antioch that would let all know what the church expected of non-Jewish converts to Christianity (Acts 15:22). A few verses down we find him identified as a "prophet" in his own right (verse 32). Subsequently, after Paul and Barnabas quarreled, Paul chose Silvanus as his chief assistant for his second missionary tour (Acts 15:39-41). He would eventually arrive in Rome, where he served as Peter's secretary and was responsible for penning 1 Peter (1 Peter 5:12). In the meantime, he had joined Paul in the founding of the Thessalonian church (Acts 17:4).

Timothy appears for the first time in Acts 16:1-5 when Paul requested his assistance on his second missionary tour. Thus Timothy became part of the evangelistic team that first entered Thessalonica. Paul would come to see him as a spiritual son (1 Cor. 4:17; 1 Tim. 1:2; 2 Tim. 1:2) as well as a fellow worker (Rom. 16:21). Because he had great confidence in Timothy, he dispatched him on various missions to the young congregations he had founded (Acts 19:22; 1 Cor. 4:17; 16:10; Phil. 2:19). The apostle would do the same when he feared for the church at Thessalonica and desired news of their spiritual health (1 Thess. 3:2, 6).

The above biographical information indicates that both Silvanus and Timothy were serving as Paul's assistants during the founding of the church at Thessalonica. "Assistants" is the key word in that sentence. While Paul never worked alone, E. Randolph Richards points to an interesting distinction when he notes that the apostle had two types of collaborators—men such as Barnabas and Luke, who were his peers, and those such as Timothy and Silvanus, who were his assistants. The interesting fact in that distinction is that in the seven letters in which Paul includes his companions in his salutations, it is always the assistants who are listed and never his peers. As a result, Richards convincingly argues, "Paul's letters were a team project, but not a team of near-equals. Paul was the leader and the dominant voice; the others were his disciples" (Richards, p. 33). We can conclude therefore that Paul was the author of the letter, and that the others were in harmony with its content. The first person singular pronoun ("I") at crucial junctures in the letter (1 Thess. 2:18; 3:5; 5:27) clearly indicates that fact even though the "we" pronouns dominate the text.

The letter is addressed "to the church of the Thessalonians *in* God the Father and the Lord Jesus Christ." The verse raises several important issues. First is the nature of the community itself. Paul calls it the *ekklēsia* or church, a common Greek word for an assembly of citizens or for a society of people who share common beliefs (see Bauer, pp. 303, 304). The Greek translators of the Old Testament used *ekklēsia* for *qahal*, which referred to the congregation of Israel. Thus *ekklēsia* was an excellent word choice for the church.

But the church, Paul tells us, is a gathering or *ekklēsia* of a unique type. It is "*in* God the Father and the Lord Jesus Christ." Its participants were no longer merely members of Greco-Roman culture or of the Jewish community, but of a new community called out of the larger culture and identified with God and Jesus Christ. To be part of a community in God, Chrysostom (c. 347-407) pointed out, "is a great dignity, and to which there is nothing equal" (*Nicene,* vol. 13, p. 324). With that insight he has captured the tremendous truth of what it means to be a Christian—to be one of those called out of the world into fellowship with the Father and the Son. Thus the Christian church is a unique entity in world history.

But, we need to ask, what does Paul mean when he writes that the church is "in" the Father and Jesus Christ? Two major possibilities surface. One is that the church exists in the atmosphere of the divine and that day by day all a Christian's deeds are done in God. A second is that the believer's salvation lies in what God accomplished by Christ's life, death, and resurrection. Both alternatives are true.

William Barclay highlights one aspect of that picture when he writes that "God was the very atmosphere in which the Church lived and moved and had its being. Just as the air is in us, and we are in the air, and we cannot live without the air, so the true Church is in God and God in the true Church, and there is no true life for the Church without God" (Barclay, pp. 216, 217).

The next important phrase we want to examine is "God the Father." For Paul, God is not merely an austere being who created the world and will someday judge it. To the contrary, to those in relationship to Him, He is "Father." Thus the Thessalonian Christians who are suffering under persecution and perhaps separation from their family now have a new family (the church) with a new Father who cares for them in parental love. One of the important functions of Jesus' ministry had been to help His followers grasp the fact that God is "our Father" (Matt. 6:9). The fathership of God also implies a sibling relationship among those who follow Him in Christ. Thus Paul addresses the Thessalonians as brothers and sisters (1 Thess. 2:1; 4:1).

The good news is that as Christians we are part of God's family. We, like the Thessalonians of old, may have turned away from the world and its ways, but we are not alone. Because we belong to the *ekklēsia* of God in Christ, we have God as our Father, the Son as our sibling, and a host of other brothers and sisters in the church who share our values, goals, and dreams of the future.

Another important word combination in 1 Thessalonians 1:1 is "Jesus Christ." Most of us think of those words merely as the name of a person. But they are much more than that. Jesus Christ was never Jesus' name on earth. Rather, He was known as Jesus of Nazareth. The four Gospels, of course, refer to Him as Jesus Christ, but that is in retrospect (many years after Paul wrote to the Thessalonians), after the church had recognized His divinity. Thus Matthew 1:16 can refer to Jesus at His birth as the one "who is called Christ" (RSV), and Peter's great revelation is that Jesus was "the Christ, the Son of the living God" (Matt. 16:16, RSV).

"The Christ" was the way a first-century Jew would have thought of the term, because it is the Greek translation of "the Messiah" in Hebrew. The word in both languages means "the annointed one," the one who was to fulfill Israel's expectation of a deliverer. Only gradually as Jesus ministered to His followers did they begin to see Him as "the Christ," the one that God had sent to fulfill the redemptive role of the Messiah in a unique way through His life and death. More revolutionary yet was the linking of Jesus the Messiah with His divinity. But it is that insight that represented the breakthrough in Peter's understanding when he linked Jesus' being the Christ to His being the Son of God in Matthew 16:16. That same connection appears in Jesus' birth narrative in Matthew 1:23, which identifies Jesus the Christ as "Emmanuel" or "God with us." Only later did Christ become "the personal name ascribed to Jesus" (Bauer, p. 1091).

As a result, when 1 Thessalonians 1:1 refers to Jesus Christ it is making a statement about Him that sets forth the idea that He is both human (Jesus) and divine (Christ). The word "Lord" flashes forth that same truth. Once again we are using a word rich in history to both Jew and Gentile. The Jew saw the word "Lord" (*kurios*) in terms of the Septuagint (the Greek translation of the Hebrew Bible), in which it was the name for God. Gentile readers would have had a similar sense, since in the pagan world

Who Is Jesus?

1. He is Jesus of Nazareth, His human name.
2. He is the Christ, God's anointed deliverer and redeemer, identified in the Gospels as the divine Son of God.
3. He is "the Lord," the very word used for God in the Jewish translation of the Old Testament.
4. He is presented in 1 Thessalonians 1:1 as both divine and human. Or as Matthew 1:23 puts it, Jesus is "God with us."

"lord" also had the overtones of deity.

Thus when Paul said that the church was not only in the Father but also in "the Lord Jesus Christ," he was making the very highest claim of divinity for Jesus, one that put Him equal to the Father. The rest of 1 Thessalonians reinforces that perspective. As a result, we find God the "Father" and "our Lord Jesus" linked together as a plural subject with a singular verb as the object of prayer in 1 Thessalonians 3:11. Paul presents the Father and Jesus Christ as equal members in the divine Godhead. Truly we Christians who are "in God the Father and the Lord Jesus Christ" have a unique heritage and an outstanding blessing.

The final words of 1 Thessalonian's greeting are also packed with meaning: "Grace to you and peace." Grace, of course, is one of Paul's favorite words, representing God's free gift of salvation through Christ. And peace, from the Hebrew *shalom*, is also central to his theology. The peace of which he speaks is not merely the absence of war but a profound sense of well-being that comes from being right with God.

Gordon Fee makes a helpful suggestion when he notes that the word order in verse 1 is of special importance. The Greek order of "Grace to you and peace" rather than the translation of most versions as "grace and peace to you" has a significant message for us. Namely, "the grace of God and Christ is what is given to God's people; peace is what results from such a gift." Therefore, "the sum total of God's activity toward his human creatures is found in the word 'grace,'" and "the sum total of those benefits as they are experienced by the recipients of God's grace is 'peace.' . . . The latter (peace) flows out of the former (grace), and both together come from 'God our Father' and are made effective in our human history through our 'Lord Jesus Christ'" (Fee, *Thessalonians*, pp. 17, 18). Amen! Not a bad beginning for a pastoral letter of comfort and hope.

Part II

Personal Matters

1 Thessalonians 1:2-3:13

2. Encouraging Words to a Faithful Church

1 Thessalonians 1:2-5a

²We give thanks to God always for all of you, making mention of you in our prayers, ³constantly remembering before our God and Father your work of faith and labor of love and steadfastness of hope in our Lord Jesus Christ, ⁴knowing, brothers beloved by God, that He has chosen you; ⁵because our gospel did not come to you in word only, but also in power and in the Holy Spirit and in fullness of conviction.

Good start, Paul. If we want to encourage a church or an individual facing persecution and its discouraging results in their lives it is always best to begin with the positive. Uplift the best in them and provide hope for both the present and the future.

Unfortunately, many "prophets of doom" in today's church follow the exact opposite. Instead of thanksgiving, they focus on the failures of the church and its members and end up weakening them and destroying their ability to persevere. But Paul has it right. Encouraging, positive words energize and by their very content point the hearer in a healthy and constructive direction as they seek to do more and more of the same sorts of activities.

Encouraging words, of course, must be based upon facts. And so it is with Paul's in verses 2-5. The return of Timothy has brought the good news of the Thessalonians' faith and love and the fact that they have no ill will toward Paul and his evangelistic team even though they might have chosen to feel deserted and neglected by them (1 Thess. 3:6). Timothy's report was the occasion for Paul's rejoicing (verse 9) and also the writing of his first letter to them. He had seen his ongoing prayers for them abundantly answered.

The apostle's "thanks" (1 Thess. 1:2) was not a generality, but rather had three focal points:

1. The evidence of their genuine Christianity in their "work of faith and labor of love and steadfastness of hope" in Christ (verse 3).
2. That God had "chosen" them for salvation (verse 4).
3. And that the gospel had come into their lives with Spirit-driven power and conviction (verse 5).

The fact that Paul highlighted the Thessalonians' faith, love, and hope is no accident. That triad of virtues appears surprisingly often in the New Testament (Rom. 5:1-5; 1 Cor. 13:13; Gal. 5:5, 6; 1 Thess. 5:8; Col. 1:4, 5; Eph. 4:2-5; Heb. 6:10-12; 10:22-24; 1 Peter 1:3-8, 21, 22) and appears to give "expression to the whole of Christian life" (Ridderbos, p. 248), or, as Reformer John Calvin put it, provides "a brief definition of true Christianity" (Calvin, "Thessalonians," p. 239).

Ernest Best makes an important point when he observes that "in the present passage each of the triad is qualified by a word which suggests activity; the triad thus does not consist of three virtues to be contemplated but three to be expressed." Thus faith works, love labors, and hope perseveres in the face of difficulty. Best goes on to note that verse 3 is not talking about generalities but implies a "your" before each virtue and its attendant activity. It is your labor, your love, and so on for all six entities of the three pairs (Best, p. 67). As a result, Paul presents the triad of virtues in verse 3 as both active and personal. Another way of saying it is that genuine Christianity must affect the way that individuals live their new lives in Christ. Christianity is not an abstraction but a life-changing experience

> **Encouraging Words Make a Difference**
>
> "In every human being [Christ] discerned infinite possibilities. He saw men as they might be, transfigured by His grace. . . . Looking upon them with hope, He inspired hope."
>
> But "An atmosphere of unsympathetic criticism is fatal to effort" (White, *Education*, pp. 80, 291).

reflected in a person's most basic values and virtues. Paul was thankful that such had been the case in the lives of the Thessalonian believers.

But the Christian values and virtues were not merely for the Thessalonians. "Every Christian without exception is a believer, a lover and a hoper" (Stott, p. 30). An examination of each member of the triad will help us see more fully the meaning of Christianity for our lives.

The first, "your work of faith," comes as a surprise to many, who seem to have the opinion that Paul is for faith but against works. Nothing could be further from the truth. While he did claim that works have no salvific value and do not contribute to our salvation (Rom. 3:20; Eph. 2:8, 9), he repeatedly and consistently asserted that good works flow out of a person's new life in Christ. Thus in Romans, Galatians, and Ephesians, the first half of each book deals with the gospel of salvation by grace, while the second half treats how that saving grace should affect believers' daily life as they walk in the will and ways of God. For Paul, works flow out of faith and a saved relationship to God. Christians do not work to get saved, but because they have been saved. The apostle has no doubt that good works have resulted from faith in the Thessalonian believers. For that he is thankful.

The second member of the triad is love that labors. Jesus put love at the very center of the Christian life and God's law when He taught that loving God with all one's mind and heart and loving one's neighbor as one's self stood at the core of the Judeo-Christian ethic (Matt. 22:34-40). That love, of course, is not an abstraction. Rather, it exerts itself in caring labor for others, reflecting what God has done for lost sinners in Christ. Paul sums up the idea nicely in Galatians 5:14, in which he writes of "faith working through love" (RSV). The apostle is thankful that such laboring and sacrificing love is a reality in the Thessalonian church (1 Thess. 4:10; cf. 2 Cor. 8:1-5).

Hope, the third member of the triad, was especially pertinent in Thessalonica because of the intense persecution the believers had been experiencing from the very founding of their church (1 Thess. 2:14). They had never known any kind of Christianity but the persecuted variety. Their experience was hardly that of the gospel of wealth "sold" by some television evangelists.

The thankful news is that the Thessalonian believers, although new in the faith and without proper pastoral support, had not caved in to the persecuting and discriminating pressures that had engulfed them. Their hope had remained steadfast.

That takes strong hope. And it is exactly what they had. It was a hope based upon the return of the resurrected Jesus who would deliver them from both their present circumstances and wrath at the end of time (1 Thess. 1:10). The letter depicts those without such assurance as being without hope (1 Thess. 4:13).

If the triad of virtues provides Paul with a first reason for giving thanks to God for the church at Thessalonica, their chosenness is a second (1 Thess. 1:4). Chosenness here does not indicate that God has predestinated some people for salvation and others for damnation. Rather, it means that God chose to send His Son so that "whoever believes in him should not perish but have eternal life" (John 3:16, RSV). It is that same love for the world found in John 3:16 that the apostle gives as the basis for God's choosing the Thessalonian believers. The ground of their election is that they were "beloved by God" (1 Thess. 1:4).

God's love has always formed the basis of His election. From the time of His searching for lost Adam in the Garden (Gen. 3:8, 9), the Bible pictures the God of love exerting Himself to rescue sinners. Or, as Abraham Joshua Heschel puts it, "All of human history as described in the Bible may be summarized in one phrase: *God is in search of man*. Faith in God is a response to God" (Heschel, p. 136).

The Thessalonians have made that faith choice and are thus included in God's chosen. For that, Paul is thankful (1 Thess. 1:2). In 1 Thessalonians 1:3 and 5 the apostle provides two pieces of evidence for his assertion that the members of the Thessalonian church have been "chosen." The first is they have demonstrated their chosenness through living lives of working faith, laboring love, and persevering hope (verse 3). The second is that their lives witness to the fact that the gospel had transformed them (cf. Rom. 12:2) "in power and in the Holy Spirit" (1 Thess. 1:5). They had given up the ways of the world and were accepting those of Christ through the power of the Spirit. In short, Paul knew they were among the elect because of their lives. They had not only been born of the water, but also of the Spirit (see John 3:3-5) and their behavior demonstrated that fact.

Before moving away from 1 Thessalonians 1:5, we should note Paul's careful balance between receiving the word from God and its practical outcome in a believer's life. He was very precise when he penned that "our gospel did not come to you in word only, but also in power and in the Holy Spirit and in fullness of conviction."

The apostle could be certain that the gospel had come to the Thessalonians by the Word, but not by the "word only." Here we have a vital distinction. First, the words of the apostles are important because they provide believers with the content of God's good news. But that verbal content is not something merely for the head. It must be put into practice. On the other hand, practice without the safeguard, guidance, and boundary markers of the apostolic word soon loses its direction. As David Jackman so nicely phrases it, if we neglect the apostolic word and its teachings "we shall lose the heart of our message and end up with a 'gospel' which is largely lacking content and which will not produce Christian disciples" (Jackman, p. 36). Such a probability is one of the greatest threats that the church faces in the postmodern, relativistic, experience-demanding, doctrinal downplaying world of the twenty-first century.

3. Encouraging Words to an Active, Waiting Church

1 Thessalonians 1:5b-10

*5b*Just as you know what kind of men we were among you for your sake, *6*so also you became imitators of us and of the Lord, having received the word in much affliction with joy from the Holy Spirit, *7*so that you became an example to all those believing in Macedonia and in Achaia. *8*For the word of the Lord has rang out from you, not only in Macedonia and in Achaia, but your faith in God has gone out everywhere, so that we have no need to say anything. *9*For they themselves report about us what sort of welcome we had from you, and how you turned to God from idols to serve a living and true God, *10*and to wait for His Son from heaven, whom He raised from the dead, Jesus the one who saves us from the wrath to come.

Paul seemingly can't find enough good things to say about the Thessalonian church. His list began in verse 2 and it plows right on until verse 10. In verses 5b-10 he pictures the congregation as

1. an imitative church (verses 5, 6),
2. a joyful church in the midst of persecution (verse 6),
3. an exemplary church that spread the gospel message (verses 7-9),
4. a converted church (verses 9, 10), and
5. a waiting church (verse 10).

Imitation can be good or bad, helpful to one's Christian experience or destructive. It all depends upon one's role model. In Paul's opinion, the Thessalonians had followed a healthy model. How could he think otherwise? After all, he writes to them, "you became imitators of us and of the Lord" (verse 6).

At first glance the word order in that statement seems out of order. Shouldn't the primary imitation be following the example of Christ or God? It should be, but the divine model was not immediately available and no New Testament or written Gospels existed at this early date. The example of the missionaries was all they had to go by. The apostolic team had been preaching by both their words and their lives.

Fortunately, the apostle himself had been following a good model. Gordon Fee helps us grasp the full implications of imitation in Christian living when he writes that "Paul's calling on his converts elsewhere to 'imitate' him as he 'imitated' Christ is the key to the ethical instructions given in his churches, where they have no 'book' to follow. 1 Corinthians 11:1 provides the starting point: Paul considered himself a follower of the example and teaching of Christ; his following Christ then served as a 'model' for his churches, who in turn, as verse 7 in our present passage makes clear, became 'models' for others" (Fee, p. 38).

A part of the imitative experience of the Thessalonian Christians had been forced upon them. Just as Paul had experienced persecution in

The Flow of Christian Imitation

1. Christ the real model
2. His witnesses, who extend the model
3. Their converts, who continue the process as they become witnesses

Thessalonica (Acts 17:5), so had the new believers (1 Thess. 1:6; Acts 17:6). They were dealing with an especially violent group of Jews who not only inflamed the local Gentiles (1 Thess. 2:14) and drove Paul out of Thessalonica, but followed him to Berea, where they soon stimulated aggression among the people there (Acts 17:13). The hostility spilled over to Paul's converts from the very beginning of the founding of the church in Thessalonica.

> "The degree in which the believer is allowed to participate in the sufferings of his Lord, should be the measure of his joy" (Lightfoot, p. 14).

The remarkable thing about their persecution is that it was accompanied by joy from the Holy Spirit (1 Thess. 1:6). That was undoubtedly a part of their imitation of Paul and his evangelistic colleagues. Joy in the midst of tribulation is as old as Christianity itself. Jesus set the stage when He said "blessed are those who are persecuted for righteousness' sake" (Matt. 5:10, RSV) and when He commanded His followers to "leap for joy" when they suffered on account of Him (Luke 6:23, RSV). That teaching was demonstrated in the early post-Pentecost church when after being physically beaten for preaching their faith the apostles went out "rejoicing that they were counted worthy to suffer dishonor" for Christ's name (Acts 5:41, RSV). Paul modeled that same joy when he wrote to the church at Colossae that "I rejoice in my sufferings for your sake" (Col. 1:24, RSV).

First Thessalonians 1:7 indicates that Paul's example was not only reflected in the Thessalonians living joyfully under stress, but also in their missionary outreach. Being at one of the crossroads of the Roman Empire (see introduction), they were well placed to influence the Greek world. And Paul rejoiced that they did not fail to exploit their missionary possibilities. By the time he writes, this new congregation had taken the gospel message into both Macedonia and Achaia (modern Greece). "The word of the Lord," Paul enthuses, "has rang out from you" (verse 8). The Greek word translated as "rang" is used in other places to describe a clap of thunder, the cry of a multitude, the blast of a trumpet, and a rumor that spreads everywhere. The verb's perfect tense indicates ongoing activity and probably lasting effect (Rogers, p. 472; Green, p. 101). Their ringing message, in fact, was so forceful that Paul writes that because of the Thessalonians' evangelistic outreach he did not find it necessary to preach in certain places. They had done it for him, and apparently done it well (1 Thess. 1:8).

Part of their evangelistic message had been their own conversion story. And a forceful one it was. Verses 9 and 10 "give a three-part analysis of Christian conversion, which is arguably the fullest account of it in the New Testament" (Stott, p. 38). The first part of their conversion was that they "turned to God," "a living and true God," the God who is active in the affairs of the world and the church, the creator God who can make a difference in our lives, as opposed to a deity who is the creation of our imaginations and is both powerless and nonexistent.

But to turn toward something is to turn away from something else. Thus a second aspect of their conversion story was their abandonment of idols. The Thessalonians had experienced conversion in the New Testament sense of a radical reorientation of the heart and life to a new set of beliefs, values, and goals. Such an experience accepted no compromise or "syncretism between their new faith and old religious loyalties" (Green, p. 106). It represented a clean break with the past and a new way of life. With that radical departure from their past with its idol worship went a forsaking of the immoral practices associated with such worship (cf. 1 Peter 4:3).

Given the fact that religion had political, social, and economic ties, conversion was not merely a private matter, but one that had deeply affected every aspect of the new believers' lives. Undoubtedly, their abandonment of idols and the emperor cult had caused the social tensions and the resulting persecution that had inundated the new converts in Thessalonica. The surrounding culture viewed them as being both unpatriotic and unfaithful. And, even more serious, such attitudes and practices could lead to a loss of economic and political privileges by the city itself.

While their shift from the worship of idols to the worship of "a living and true God" (1 Thess. 1:9) triggered persecution, it also brought joy (verse 6). And that joy was tied to the third aspect of their conversion. They were now no longer merely living for the moment, but waiting for the return of Jesus (verse 10). Their hope was built on the promise of His second advent, at which time their salvation would be complete. That topic, which they did not yet fully understand, will show up in every chapter of 1 and 2 Thessalonians. Their need of instruction about the Second Coming will provide us with some of the most helpful teachings on it in the entire Bible.

One of the sad facts of Christian history is that the very topic that provided the basis of hope for first-century believers has been lost sight of by many religious leaders and their followers. Leon Morris writes that "the prominence given to the second coming is in sharp contrast to so much that calls itself Christianity in modern times. This doctrine is mentioned most frequently of all [doctrines] in the New Testament, there being, so I am told, a reference to it on the average once every thirteen verses from Matthew right through to Revelation. Its neglect in many quarters is something which cannot be countenanced from Scripture" (Morris, *First and Second*, 1959, p. 64). Paul is so excited about the prospect of Christ's return that he calls it "our blessed hope" (Titus 2:13).

That hope, of course, rests upon the person of Jesus, whom the apostle describes in verse 10 as God's "Son from Heaven," the one who has been "raised from the dead," and "the one who saves us from the wrath to come," when the God who will not let the destructive results of sin go on forever finally in His love puts an end to a broken world and its ongoing misery (Rev. 19; 20). The Bible describes that time of the righting of wrongs as one of fear for those in rebellion against God (Rev. 6:15-17), but one of promise for the children of God. In fact, it is that very foundation hope that strengthened the Thessalonian believers in their time of tribulation. And it will do the same for God's people until the end of history. The full gospel (good news) of the New Testament is not only that Jesus died for sinners and rose again, but that He will come again and take His people home.

4. Words of Defense: A Faithful Pastor

1 Thessalonians 2:1-4
[1]For you yourselves know, brothers, that our visit to you has not been in vain, [2]but having previously suffered and been mistreated in Philippi, as you know, we had courage in our God to speak to you the good news of

God amid much opposition. ³For our exhortation does not come from error or impurity or with deceit, ⁴but just as we have been approved by God to be entrusted with the gospel, so we speak, not to please people, but God, who tests our hearts.

It is of more than passing interest that Paul's earliest letters devote more space to a defense of his ministry than does his later correspondence. Thus we find him in Galatians (written about the same time as 1 Thessalonians) providing an extensive vindication of his apostleship and the validity of his approach to the gospel. We find a similar justification in 1 Thessalonians, but here it is not his apostleship that is in question but his character and his motives.

We wonder why the early Paul spends so much time in self-defense. It may be that he had not yet established his credentials as a faithful messenger in the Roman world, whereas his later letters rested upon a proven track record and an established reputation. Although we will never know all the reasons, we can be thankful for the priceless information that his defenses provide about the earliest Christian congregations in the Greek world and the problematic context in which they existed, in terms of both Jewish and Gentile opposition. Another benefit is the biographical information that they offer.

One of the major contributions of the second and third chapters of 1 Thessalonians is the insight they give us into Paul's pastoral heart. "In these chapters, more perhaps than anywhere else in his letters, he discloses his mind, expresses his emotions and bares his soul" (Stott, p. 45). As he does he offers many helpful insights into the meaning of pastoral ministry.

We need to read Paul's defense and his deep concern for the Thessalonian church in the light of the history of his relationship with the congregation. Acts 17:1-10 relates his brief ministry to them, his remarkable success in obtaining converts, and the attack by the Jewish leaders that drove him out of the city in a humiliating night flight even before he had fully indoctrinated the new members.

Paul's enemies lost no time in exploiting his sudden exit. By examining the apostle's defense in 1 Thessalonians we discover that their approach aimed at discrediting him in the eyes of his converts. Included in the charges against him were claims that he had deserted his followers as soon as things got difficult, that he must not care about the new Christians in Thessalonica since they hadn't heard anything from him, and that he had arrived in the first place to take advantage of whoever would listen to him. In short, the accusations implied, Paul was just one more opportunistic travelling teacher who was out to milk gullible people for whatever they were worth, that he didn't really care about them, that he took off and deserted them to face adversity alone as soon as things got difficult.

The problem was that the basic scenario looked plausible. As a result, Paul feared that the new converts might believe the accusations and turn against the gospel. In fact, from the tone of the letter it seems likely that some of them were beginning to doubt his motives and integrity.

His defense in 1 Thessalonians was important to Paul not so much for the accusations against him as a person, but because the future of the gospel and the Thessalonian congregation was in jeopardy. His response to the charges falls into two parts: 1 Thessalonians 2:1-16 presents an explanation of his conduct in Thessalonica and 1 Thessalonians 2:17-3:13 explains his sudden departure from them, his inability to return, and his determination to visit them as soon as he can.

The first part of Paul's explanation is a clarification of his motives. Verse 2 faces the issue of his "cowardice." The fact that he preached openly in Thessalonica after his suffering and shameful treatment at Philippi, he asserts, puts the lie to that accusation.

The words that Paul uses to describe his treatment at Philippi reveal the depth of his pain and humiliation there. Acts 16 portrays how he and Silas were dragged before the rulers, attacked by the crowd, stripped of their clothes by the magistrates, beat with "many blows," and thrown into the inner prison, with their feet bound in stocks (verses 19-24).

Needless to say, it is a bit humiliating to be flogged naked in public. Paul hadn't forgotten the suffering and mistreatment (1 Thess. 2:2). While the suffering was difficult, the word he uses for mistreatment exposes his forceful emotions on the topic and the depth of his humiliation. It is a word that "expresses insulting and outrageous treatment, and esp[ecially] treatment which is calculated publicly to insult and openly to humiliate the person who suffers from it" (Rogers, pp. 472, 473). It had had its effect, and Paul was still smarting from it when he arrived in Thessalonica.

Yet, in spite of the excruciating experience in Philippi, Paul points out in 1 Thessalonians 2:2: "we had courage in our God to speak to you the good news of God amid much opposition." Thus exhibit number one is on the table: Paul is not a coward. It took guts to enter into the fray again right after the Philippian experience when the physical and emotional wounds had not yet healed.

At this point we should note the last word in verse 2. I have translated it as "opposition" because that is one meaning of the word and, according to Acts 17, it fits the facts of what actually happened. But the Greek word "*agōn*" also implies strenuous effort or conflict in which the English word "agony" is implied. That side of the word highlights even more Paul's emotional state as he preached the gospel in Thessalonica in spite of his wounded psyche.

The apostle summons the Thessalonians themselves as first-person, authoritative witnesses to his courage. That is the significance of the "you know" in 1 Thessalonians 2:2. Five times in verses 1-10 Paul refers to them as witnesses. Beyond that, he calls upon God twice as a character witness.

"*You yourselves know*" that our visit to you "has not been in vain" (verse 1).

"*You know*" we had courage" (verse 2).

"*You know*" we never used flattering. "*God is our witness*" (verse 5, RSV).

"*You remember*" (verse 9, RSV).

"*You are witnesses*, and *God also*" (verse 10, RSV).

The repeated call for witnesses is an appeal to facts established on the basis of Paul's public activities. Those events, to which the Thessalonians themselves were witnesses, disprove the accusations of the critics.

First Thessalonians 2:3 launches the next step in Paul's response to his attackers. Reflecting the words of the accusers, Paul claims that his message and motives did not come from error, impurity, or deceit. The background behind those accusations that would have given them plausibility in the first-century Greek world is that there were at that time a large number of traveling teachers circulating among the cities with their various philosophic and religious ideas. Their aim was to gain disciples and thereby develop a financial base that would free them from the necessity of gainful employment. Such teachers cared more for themselves than their hearers, who in actuality were only important to them as sources of money, sex, and prestige. It is against that background that we need to read Paul's ongoing defense in chapter 2.

In the face of such charlatans, Paul asserts that his teaching did not spring from error, but was genuine good news from God. Beyond that, it was not associated with impurity. While impurity is most often linked with sex, as it was with many of the traveling "evangelists" of his day, the meaning here is undoubtedly the wider connotation of impure motives, such as ambition, pride, greed, or popularity. Finally, his message was not related to deceit. Here we have a word meaning to bait a trap, so that an animal would think it was getting something good only to be tricked (Bauer, p. 256; Thayer, 155). Such was the practice of the false wandering teachers in Paul's day, who were "peddling their religious or philosophical nostrums, and living at the expense of their devotees" (Bruce, p. 26).

But it was not so with Paul. He sets forth his reputation in verse 4. His "preaching could not have proceeded from error, for he was entrusted by God with the message. He was not impure, for he had been approved by God. He was not a trickster, for he aimed at pleasing God, not people" (Morris, *First and Second*, 1991, p. 63). Reinforcing that defense, of course, was the personal witness of the Thessalonian believers.

Blessed is the religious leader and church member who has nothing to hide, who in all sincerity can call upon both God and those in the church and even the larger community to testify to their uprightness and purity of motives. May their tribe increase.

5. Words of Defense: Ministry as Loving Mother

1 Thessalonians 2:5–8

⁵For we never used words of flattery, as you know, nor did we come with a cloak for greed, as God is witness, ⁶nor did we seek glory from men, either from you or from others, though as apostles of Christ we could have been a burden to you. ⁷But we were gentle among you, just as a nursing mother takes care of her own children. ⁸So being affectionately desirous of you, we were pleased to share with you not only the gospel of God but also our own lives, because you had become very dear to us.

One of the major contributions of 1 Thessalonians 2:1–12 is "its apostolic definition of what authentic gospel ministry is all about and in the picture that is painted of an authentic gospel minister" (Jackman, p.

51). Paul's exposition began in verses 1-4 with his description of the faithful pastor as one whose message is true, motives are pure, and methods are open and above reproach. Verses 5-8 move the discussion forward by picturing ministry in terms of the loving, caring, and self-giving mother, while verses 9-12 focus on the upright father who instructs and encourages.

While some people might be tempted to see those lessons as applying to their pastor, we might better view them as the characteristics of each of us as Christians, since we all minister to one another. Of course, they do provide the church with criteria for evaluating professional clergy in terms of biblical adequacy.

First Thessalonians 2:5-8 approaches the topic of Paul's ministry from two directions: a negative in verses 5 and 6, and a positive in verses 7 and 8. The first thing Paul tells us in verse 5 is that he and his colleagues never employed flattery as an evangelistic tool. Here we find a much used tactic among the self-serving traveling teachers of the ancient Greek world. The word itself "carries with it the idea of the tortuous methods by which one man seeks to gain influence over another, generally for his own ends, and when we keep in view the selfish conduct of too many of the heathen rhetoricians of the day . . . we can easily understand how such a charge might come to be laid against the Apostles" (Moulton, p. 352). It is no accident that we find an allusion to greed in the same verse. The apostolic team in Thessalonica, Paul asserts, did not stoop to such strategies.

Neither, he adds in a second negative statement, did they arrive with a cloak for greed. A cloak, of course, is a garment. The meaning here is that Paul "had never misused his apostolic office in order to disguise or to hide avaricious designs" (Thayer, p. 552) as did so many of the religious and philosophical teachers of his day.

Here we find a problem that has existed all through the church's history—unethical preachers cloaked in sheep's clothing but with the greedy heart of a wolf (Matt. 7:15). One only has to think of that extremely profitable TV ministry of some years ago identified as PTL. That acronym stood for "Praise the Lord," but after the arrest of its leadership for bilking viewers out of tens of millions of dollars PTL became caricatured as "Pass the Loot." In his defense to the Thessalonians, Paul distances himself from all who would use ministry as a cloak or cover for avarice. To the contrary, he will focus on ministry as giving rather than getting (1 Thess. 2:7).

The apostle's third negative description of ministry is that it must not be glory seeking (verse 6). In the days before Hollywood, television, and modern sports, one of the most popular ways to achieve the praise of others was through oratory. But Paul is clear that all glory and praise belong to God rather than to His followers.

The final negative point is that the apostolic team did not become a burden to the Thessalonians (verse 6). The Greek word translated as "burden" has at least two possible meanings in the text, both found in various English translations. The first is to become an economic drain to the church. That was not Paul's approach. He will point out in verse 9 that they toiled night and day that they might not be a liability.

The alternative translation of the Greek word for burden appears in the Revised Standard Version, which reads *barei* as "demands." The sense in that translation is that the evangelistic team could have used their weighty apostolic authority in a self-important manner. Once again the context supplies support for the translation, with verse 7 suggesting that their approach to the new converts was "gentle" rather than demanding. As is often the case in Paul's writings, he may be implying both meanings.

Thus far in our discussion we have examined a list of the negative attributes to watch out for in a person claiming to be God's messenger. To put it bluntly, beware of them if they utilize flattery, are greedy and overly interested in money, seek praise for themselves, are more willing to suck up the resources of the church than to contribute to them, or are demanding and authoritative. Jesus was quick to point out that not everything that claims to be a sheep is genuine mutton (Matt. 7:15).

First Thessalonians 2:7, 8 move from the negative side of Paul's description of his ministry to the positive. "We were gentle among you, just as a nursing mother takes care of her own children." Far from being greedy, arrogant, or a burden to the church, Paul and his associates were caring in their approach to the Thessalonians. Verse 7 is not the only New Testament passage in which he presents the ministry-as-mother model. In Galatians 4:19, for example, he writes of his converts as "my dear children, for whom I am again in the pains of childbirth until Christ is formed in you" (NIV). And to the Corinthian church, he declared, "I could not speak to you as spiritual people, but rather as people of the flesh, as infants in Christ. I fed you with milk, not solid food" (1 Cor. 3:1, 2, NRSV).

The apostle sets forth the maternal aspect of ministry with the word *trophos* (employed only here in the New Testament), which is primarily used in secular Greek to refer to a wet-nurse (Bauer, p. 1017), a woman hired not only to suckle a baby, but also to care for it and even provide for its education. But *trophos* can also mean mother, which is the case in 1 Thessalonians 2:7 since it speaks of the wet-nurse as caring for "her *own*

> ### The True Pastor
>
> Paul "had been accused of seeking gain and glory when he came among them; but his sole desire had been not to get but to give. . . . That is the true standard of pastoral care" (Denney, p. 76).

children." Thus Paul and his associates had "nurtured and cared for the Thessalonian believers, not as hired help, as tender as such people might be, but as a nurse would do when she cares for the fruit of her own womb. The disposition of the apostles was not to throw their weight around with these Thessalonians but to care for them tenderly and warmly" (Green, p. 128).

Verse 8, in which Paul not only reminds the Thessalonians how "very dear" they had become to the evangelistic team, but that they were "affectionately desirous" of them, expands upon that tender warmth. It had been their privilege, Paul claims, not only to share the gospel with them, but also their own souls, a word best translated in this context as "lives" or "selves."

In other words, the apostle and his friends gave everything they had to that new congregation. They really loved them from the depth of their hearts, and that love showed up in their daily relationship to them. The Thessalonians knew that Paul cared, that he was not merely one more traveling evangelist seeking to add a few more stars to his ministerial crown. They had responded in kind to become one of Paul's flagship churches, in spite of the relatively short time that he had spent with them. Because they knew that Paul cared, it made all the difference in the world to those young believers. It gave them courage to stand for their faith even in the midst of discrimination and persecution.

In the maternal aspect of ministry we find one of its core qualities. Paul did not stand apart from his people. To the contrary, "with the delivery of his message he delivered his heart." James Clarke points out that "all changers of lives have been men who have mingled themselves with their truth" (J. Clarke, p. 273). Thus it was with Jesus, who was moved with compassion as He spoke to the people. And they responded to Him gladly (Mark 12:37; Luke 8:40). And it was the case with Jozef de Veuster (better known as Father Damien) who ministered to the lepers in Hawaii, not by remaining at a distance from them as loathsome untouchables, but by living among them, eventually accepting their leprosy into his own body, and later dying in their midst at the age of 49 as one who cared enough to give his life up so that he might share the good news of eternal life with them. The response was phenomenal as men, women, and children who had absolutely no hope in life found the only true hope. How? Through a man who truly cared and was willing to give his life rather than merely words.

I recall a statement to the effect that if we wish to do good to souls, our success will be proportionate to their understanding of our love and care for them. Adopting the maternal role of ministry is essential for both "professional clergy" and all of the rest of us who belong to the family of God. We are all to be "affectionately desirous" of others and their welfare as we share both the truth of God and our own lives with those both outside and inside of the church. That is not merely one form of Christian ministry. It is the only type. Of course, as we will see in our next Bible passage, ministry does have a paternal side.

6. Words of Defense: Ministry as Exhorting Father

1 Thessalonians 2:9-12

⁹For you remember, brothers, our labor and hardship. We worked night and day so as not to be a burden to any one of you while we proclaimed to you the gospel of God. ¹⁰You are witnesses, and God also, how devoutly and uprightly and blamelessly we behaved to you believers. ¹¹You know how we were as a father with his children to every one of you, exhorting and encouraging and charging you ¹²to walk worthy of God, the one calling you into His own kingdom and glory.

The word "for" at the beginning of both verse 5 and verse 9 ties together Paul's argument in 1 Thessalonians 2:1-12. Verses 1-4 asserted the genuineness of his apostolic ministry. The "for" of verse 5 leads into a proof of that genuineness in verses 5-8, climaxing with a statement of the evangelistic team's profound motherly love for the Thessalonian believers that led them to give their very lives for the converts they had brought into the world.

The "for" in verse 9 has a twofold reference. Most immediately, it provides more evidence of that self-giving love as witnessed by their perpetual labor to earn a living even as they gave them the gospel. But, even more foundational to the structure of verses 1-12, the "for" of verse 9 harks back to verse 4 and provides another round of demonstration on the genuineness of their apostolic ministry. But in verses 9-12 Paul changes the metaphor from motherhood to fatherhood.

James Denney helps us begin to see the significance of the shift when he indicates that true ministry includes "not only the tender fondness of a mother's [love], but the educative wisdom of a father's" (Denney, p. 77). First Thessalonians 2:9-12 sets forth the father's educational role in two ways, with verses 9 and 10 focusing on that of example, and verses 11 and 12 on that of teacher.

"You remember," Paul writes to his converts, how "we worked night and day so as not to be a burden to any one of you while we proclaimed to you the gospel of God" (verse 9). That is an interesting statement, since "in the Greek world manual labour was generally despised and travelling teachers were graded in terms of their prestige by how good a living they made out of it. So, if you were actually working away, night and day, tent-making, what you were saying to the Greek world was that your message and methods were inferior because you could not actually make a living out of it" (Jackman, p. 61).

Further complicating the situation, in other places Paul tells us in no uncertain terms that he had a right to be remunerated for his work as a minister for God (1 Cor. 9:9, 12-14; 2 Thess. 3:9). In fact, at times he received wages or "pay" (Moffatt) from his converts (2 Cor. 11:8). Even while at Thessalonica he had accepted financial help more than once from the church in Philippi (Phil. 4:16). If all those things are true, we need to ask, why did he choose to work "night and day" while evangelizing in

Thessalonica? The answer appears to be threefold. One reason shows up in 1 Thessalonians 2:9, in which Paul indicates that they did not wish to be a burden while they were delivering the gospel to them. That point refers us back to verse 8, which proclaimed Paul's undying love for his converts and the giving of the missionaries' very lives for the new believers. Their taxing labor was a demonstration of those assertions.

Another reason for their labor is hinted at in verse 10, in which Paul claims that he and his fellow ministers had behaved "uprightly and blamelessly" toward the new believers. Here we have a possible side reference to those false teachers who fleeced their gullible flocks. Some had apparently accused the apostle of being such a parasitic teacher, and he desired to put as much distance as possible between himself and those less than helpful models.

A third reason for Paul's labor was his desire to be a good example to the believers, some of whom had apparently come into the church with the Greek attitude toward manual labor and, as a result, had chosen not to work themselves (1 Thess. 5:14; 2 Thess. 3:6, 10-12). The apostle highlights the example motif again in 2 Thessalonians when he writes that "you yourselves know how you ought to imitate us; we were not idle when we were with you, we did not eat any one's bread without paying, but with toil and labor we worked night and day, that we might not burden any of you. It was not because we have not that right, but to give you in our conduct an example to imitate" (3:7-9, RSV).

We should note at this juncture that the Jewish idea of work was quite different from that of the Greeks. All young men, even those from well-to-do homes, learned a trade. Paul's was tentmaking (Acts 18:3). To counteract the Greek view of labor and to instill a Christian approach to the topic by example, we find the apostle not only working at his trade in Thessalonica but also in such places as Corinth and Ephesus (Acts 18:1-4; 20:33-35). He was strong on the role of exampleship as he led and developed the believers in the congregations he had founded.

In 1 Thessalonians 2:10 Paul goes on to assert to the church members that they were witnesses, as was God, to "how devoutly and uprightly and blamelessly" the apostolic team had behaved in their midst. I. Howard Marshall points out that "the solemnity of the tone" in that declaration "suggests strongly that Paul was dealing with real accusations that were being used by the opponents of the church to denigrate the missionaries and their message and so to turn the converts against them" (Marshall, *Thessalonians*, p. 73). To attest to the blamelessness of the apostolic team, Paul calls on both the Thessalonians themselves and God as witnesses to the truth of his claims, thus lining up with the teaching of Deuteronomy 19:15 that the validity of any claim must be attested to by two or three witnesses.

The reason that the apostle is so intent on justifying the fact that he and his preaching companions had acted uprightly in their relationship with the Thessalonians is that it was crucial that he be perceived as being what he expects them to be when he later provides them with rebuke and instruction. In short, they will need to listen to and follow his counsel because the uprightness of his life had already demonstrated his genuineness. A correct example was crucial to Paul's understanding of ministry. He knew that no one would take his teachings seriously if he did not exhibit them in his own life.

But example wasn't all that Paul had to offer in the fatherly aspect of his ministry. He also "as a father with his children" had some definite verbal instruction for them. "The father in the ancient world," Charles Wanamaker tells us, "was normally responsible for the moral instruction and behavior of his offspring." But for Paul the task was somewhat different. His was one of "resocializing his 'children in the faith' to the sometimes radically different demands of their new social existence as Christians." After all, "religious conversion requires resocialization to the distinctive ideas and values of the new religion if the convert is to be effectively incorporated into it" (Wanamaker, p. 106).

> A correct example was crucial to Paul's understanding of ministry. He knew that no one would take his teachings seriously if he did not exhibit them in his own life.

As a result, we find father Paul "exhorting and encouraging and charging" the new church members (verse 11). Here we notice three highly expressive pedagogical terms that reinforce each other. The meaning of "exhorting" is to urge a person to follow a certain line of conduct. The second term sets forth the idea of encouraging them to continue in that line of conduct. And the third, "charging," "is the strongest of the three, since it suggests the idea of insisting or requiring that a certain course of action be adopted" (Green, p. 136). Some even translate the word as "insisting." Thus Paul in his father role "demands" that his readers follow God's ways (Best, pp. 106, 107).

Such a course would result in the new church members walking "worthy of God" (verse 12). Walking for Paul is a favorite way of designating the entire conduct of one's life. Thus a person can either walk according to the values and morals of the devil or in the way of God. The two different walks of life, as we might expect, have quite diverse destinations (Rom. 8:4-7; Matt. 7:13, 14).

Here we find an important aspect of ministry all too often neglected in the twenty-first century. "Teaching on the moral life was not a secondary consideration well after this church was established, but a primary concern for its founders. Those who came into the church knew from the start what was required of them" (Green, p. 136). That is an important aspect of biblical Christianity all too often overlooked today by both church leaders and those who sit in the pews. Living the Christian life is not an option for Christians. It is at its heart.

But walking with God is not an end in itself according to 1 Thessalonians 2:12. Those who "walk worthy of God" are being called "into His own kingdom and glory." The kingdom of God in the New Testament has both present and future aspects. It came with the preaching of Jesus (Matt. 4:17), but it won't arrive in its fullness until He returns to put an end to this world of sin and to create a new heaven and earth in which the effects of sin are obliterated and in which only "righteousness dwells" (Rev. 21:1-4; 2 Peter 3:11-13, RSV).

In the meantime, God the Father is always calling His people to faithfulness, both at the beginning of their Christian walk and all through it. It is our task to accept the invitation to change life's direction and to walk daily with Him and thus be ready for the fullness of the kingdom and the glory to come.

7. Encouraging Words to a Responsive Church

1 Thessalonians 2:13-16

> *[13]For this reason we also give thanks to God constantly that when you received the word of God which you heard from us, you accepted it not as the word of men, but as what it really is, the word of God, which also is at work in you who are believing. [14]For you, brothers, became imitators of the churches of God in Christ Jesus which are in Judea, because you also suffered the same things from your own countrymen, even as they did from the Jews, [15]who killed both the Lord Jesus and the prophets, and persecuted us, and displease God and are hostile to all men, [16]hindering us from speaking to the Gentiles that they might be saved—so as always to fill up the measure of their sins. But wrath has come on them at last.*

These verses leave behind the extended defense of Paul's apostolic mission to Thessalonica (verses 1-12) and move on to treat the converts' reception of the gospel (verse 13) and the suffering they underwent as a consequence (verse 14). The passage itself represents a second round of thanksgiving for the vibrant faith of the Thessalonian believers and has many parallels with verses 5 and 6 of the first chapter.

Undergirding Paul's entire ministry is the conviction expressed in verse 13 that his message was not his own but that of God. Here he speaks of it as being the "word of God," but in other places he refers to it as the "gospel of God" (verse 9). He would later write to the believers in Corinth that he did not come to them with "lofty words" of eloquence or the "wisdom" of the philosophers, but with the "testimony of God," claiming that he had "decided to know nothing among [them] except Jesus Christ and him crucified." His preaching was not based upon philosophic "words of wisdom, but in demonstration of the Spirit and of power, that your faith might not rest in the wisdom of men but in the power of God" (1 Cor. 2:1-5, RSV). He was contented to be a conduit for the message that God had given him. And in that message was power, as we find demonstrated in the transformed lives of the Thessalonian believers.

Of course, Paul must have been tempted, as many Christians are in our day, to be "up to date" on the latest theological and philosophical trends. Leon Morris writes that "the pressure to accommodate his message to the demands of the 'modern thought-world' of the day must have been great. But Paul rejected all this. His drive and forcefulness came not from some thought that he was abreast of contemporary trends in philosophy or religion or science, but from the deep-seated conviction that he was God's mouthpiece, and that what he spoke was the veritable word of God" (Morris, *First and Second*, 1991, p. 79).

The apostle finds that same power and forcefulness in the lives of the believers in Thessalonica, who had "received the word of God which you heard" and "accepted it not as the word of men, but as what it really is, the word of God" (1 Thess. 2:13). That word of God, he goes on to note, "is at work in you who are believing." Here he is undoubtedly speaking of the dynamic "power" of the gospel message not only to save from the penalty of sin but also from its enslaving hold on human lives through the gospel's ability to transform people into new creatures (Rom. 1:16; 12:2; 2 Cor. 5:17) and to provide them with conviction, direction, and strength to face even the most difficult circumstances.

Paul had no doubt that the power of God's word was at work in the church members. When he speaks of their "believing" at the end of verse 13, he uses the present tense, indicating that belief is an ongoing process rather than something that happened in a singular way at their conversion. Thus as they continue to believe, the word of God continues to empower their lives.

One of the proofs that they had an ongoing relationship with the word of God was their constant endurance of the suffering imposed on them by their "own countrymen" (verse 14). "If it had been a merely human message, one might expect that when the hearers began to be persecuted for accepting it they would turn back and give it up. But they have not. The word has produced in them the same kind of steadfastness as that of the very first Christians, the communities of Jesus' followers in Judaea" (Wright, p. 101).

We find the roots of the persecution itself in Acts 17:5-9, which indicates that the Jews not only turned against the Christians, but that they had also excited the city leaders and the Gentiles about their teaching concerning some other king than Caesar. And with such a teaching came the fear that Rome would begin to withdraw some of the special economic and political privileges that the empire had extended to Thessalonica. The result was suffering for the believers (1 Thess. 2:14).

But Paul wants them to know that they are not alone in their experience. The earliest Christians in Judea had also endured persecution at the hands of the Jewish leaders, as did Paul himself (verse 15). By using those illustrations, the apostle desires them to understand that they are not alone in their suffering—that they belong to a widespread body of believers who will inevitably encounter persecution because of their very beliefs and allegiances (2 Tim. 3:12). Reminding individual Christians and congregations of the fact that they "belonged to a larger movement" whose members "'invoke the name of our Lord Jesus Christ in every place' (1 Cor. 1:2)" was a central purpose of Paul's writing and visiting ministries (Meeks, pp. 107-110). In the Thessalonian case, he wanted to assure them that what happened to them was not unique. Such information was not only helpful for those first-century Christians, but it has comforted suffering believers across the history of the church, and it will do so to the end of time.

First Thessalonians 2:15, 16 focus on "the Jews," whom Paul charges with six serious accusations. The first is that they "killed . . . the Lord Jesus." While it is true that the Romans actually performed the crucifixion, the Gospels leave no doubt regarding Jewish responsibility. Second, they also murdered some of their own prophets. Both the Old Testament (1 Kings 19:10, 14; Neh. 9:26) and the New (Matt. 23:31, 34, 35; Luke 11:47-51; 13:33, 34; Acts 7:52; Rom. 11:3) present the rejection and martyrdom of the prophets as serious evidence of rebellion by the Jewish nation.

A third charge is that the Jews had persecuted and driven out Paul and his colleagues. That had been true not only in Thessalonica, but by the time he wrote 1 Thessalonians it also applied to their ministry in Berea. Such would be the case in city after city as the apostles sought to preach the gospel and raise up churches (Acts 8:1; 9:28-30; 13:50; 14:5, 6; 16:39; 17:14). The book of Acts identifies many cities in which the Jews excited the populace against Paul and thus led to his expulsion (Acts 9:23-25, 29; 13:45, 50; 14:2, 4-6; 19, 20; 17:5, 13; 18:6, 12-17; 19:9; cf. 2 Cor. 11:24, 26).

Fourth, the Jews displease God, presumably because of their persecution of Christians and their blocking of the spread of the gospel message. Fifth, Paul charges them with being "hostile to all men." We need to read that broad statement in the context of his sixth accusation against the Jews: they were "hindering us from speaking to the Gentiles that they might be saved." The apostle had absolutely no doubt that his gospel message and mission were vital for the salvation of men and women. As a result, anything that blocked that mission was against humanity. And since the Jews had been fairly consistent in hindering Paul's work, he could claim that they were "hostile to all men."

Such talk makes us wonder if Paul wasn't hostile to all Jews. The answer is a resounding "no!" Far from being anti-Semitic, he devoted three precious chapters in the heart of his letter to the Romans to his love for the Jewish people and his desire for their salvation (Rom. 9-11). He concluded his appeal to them with a statement that God has provided for "mercy upon all"—both Jew and Gentile (11:32, RSV). The apostle had no doubt that the message of the gospel was for the Jews first and only then to Gentiles (Rom. 1:16). The book of Acts shows him putting that theology into practice as in city after city on his missionary tours he began his work in the Jewish synagogue before moving to the non-Jewish community.

> The suffering of the church at Thessalonica "doesn't mean that something has gone badly wrong with God's purpose for them; it means that they are on the same map as the very first churches. They are on the same map, too, as Paul himself" (Wright, pp. 101, 102).

While some may wish that Paul had been a bit more "politically correct" in his statement about the Jews, a contextual reading of his statements in 1 Thessalonians 2:15, 16 makes it clear that he was not against Jews as a people themselves, but rather the practice of all too many of them of blocking the spread of the message of salvation.

Paul closes 1 Thessalonians 2:16 with a statement that wrath "has come" on the Jews. Students of his letter are divided on its meaning. Some have applied it to the future destruction of Jerusalem in A.D. 70, but others point out the past tense of the verb and apply it to the Passover crisis of A.D. 49, in which more than 20,000 Jews perished in the Temple complex (see Josephus, *Antiquities*, 20.5.3) and the expulsion of the Jews from Rome that same year. While we may never know fully what crisis Paul had in mind, he leaves us with the definite impression that he is massively upset with those Jews who had done everything they could to destroy his work.

But the good news of verses 13-16 is not that there are problems and conflicts and suffering, but rather that such crises do not mean that we are not part of God's plan. To the contrary, enduring persecution for Christ means that we are sharing His sufferings, and that, like Him, we will some-day be vindicated.

8. Words of Concern From a Frustrated Apostle

1 Thessalonians 2:17-20

[17]But we, brothers, having been orphaned from you for a short time—in person, not in heart—were especially eager with great desire to see your face. [18]Therefore we wanted to come to you—I Paul more than once—but Satan hindered us. [19]For what is our hope or joy or crown of boasting?—Is it not even you, in the presence of our Lord Jesus at His coming? [20]For you are our glory and joy.

This paragraph puts to rest any thoughts we may have had about Paul being primarily a systematic theologian and a man focused on logic. Not so! First Thessalonians 2:17-20 pictures him as primarily a pastor, pos-sessed of a heart that throbbed with anxiety for his converts. The passage itself is charged with emotion, as the use of dashes in the translation indi-cates. The words do not flow logically and grammatically, but are filled with passion. Paul here portrays himself as a pastor who cares deeply for his children (see the mother and father images in 1 Thess. 2:7, 11).

That thought brings us to the emotionally packed word that I trans-lated as "orphaned." I had at first rendered it as "separated," and other translators utilize such expressions as "taken away from you" (NASB) or "torn away from you" (NIV), but Beverly Gaventa makes a crucial point when she says that such a rendering "explains away the metaphor and thereby reduces its impact" (Gaventa, p. 41). Greek speaking Chrysostom (c. 347-407) makes the same point when he writes that "he has not said 'separated,' but . . . much more. . . . He had said above 'as a father his chil-dren,' 'as a nurse,' here he uses another expression, 'being made orphans'" (*Nicene and Post-Nicene*, vol. 13, p. 334). And George Findlay points out that the passage employs "the very strongest expression the Apostle could find" (Findlay, p. 78).

The choice of the term "orphan" in verse 17 highlights a first-century use of the term that is different from ours. Today we employ "orphan" to indicate a child who has lost its parents, but in the New Testament world it could also apply to a parent who has lost its child. It is in that latter sense that the apostle and his colleagues had been "orphaned" from their new-born children in the faith in Thessalonica.

Acts 17 provides the backdrop for Paul's being torn away or separated or orphaned from his precious flock of believers. The Jews had got much of the city in an uproar, and friends spirited Paul and Silas away "by night" to avoid an even worse crisis in the community and even more problems for the new Christians (Acts 17:5-10).

Part of the anguish underlying the apostle's concern is that his detractors in Thessalonica had apparently accused him of not really caring for the new members. In fact, the claim went, his failure to return to help them in their time of need further demonstrated that lack of concern.

In the face of such a charge, Paul asserts that he and his colleagues may have been bodily absent from the Thessalonian Christians, but that the new believers had been much in their hearts, minds, and thoughts. We see the intensity of his emotion expressed in the phrase indicating that he and his mission team "were especially eager with great desire to see you face to face." "Eager with great desire" is an interesting phraseology since the verb "to see" has two modifiers. And in the Jewish mind to repeat something is to give it the effect of being superlative. Thus the king of kings is the greatest of all of kings and the song of songs is the greatest song. In the same way, "eager" and "great desire" express the greatest desire possible or "excessive" desire (Frame, p. 119). Paul wants the Thessalonians to know his true feelings about them in no uncertain terms.

Those sentiments were not merely thoughts. Verse 18 tells us that Paul and his team had tried to return more than once but that "Satan" had blocked them from doing so. The apostle personalizes the attempt to return by emphasizing the fact that he himself had more than once sought to do so.

The reason he hadn't been able to return is because "Satan hindered us." The word translated as "hindered" has military overtones, as when an army destroys a road "to block the way" of an invading force (Kittel, vol.

3, p. 855). Thus the passage presents a warfare imagery that stands at the heart of God's struggle with Satan in other biblical passages (see, e.g., Rev. 12). Peter expresses the intensity of the conflict when he writes that "your adversary the devil prowls around like a roaring lion, seeking some one to devour" (1 Peter 5:8, RSV). Regarding the Thessalonians, Paul feared that "the tempter had tempted" them to apostasy.

The apostle doesn't often mention the name of Satan, but in several places he reflects on his battle against Satan or "the adversary" who wages war against him and his mission (see, e.g., Rom. 16:20; 1 Cor. 7:5; 2 Cor. 2:11; 11:14; 12:7; 2 Thess. 2:9). He also labels his enemy as "the devil" (Eph. 4:27; 1 Tim. 3:6, 7), "the ruler of the kingdom of the air" (Eph. 2:2, NIV), and "the tempter" (1 Thess. 3:5). Paul has not the slightest doubt that he is dealing with a supernatural being who exemplifies the essence of an evil personality.

But he doesn't tell us how Satan prevented his return. It may have been the ongoing Jewish opposition that followed him to Berea (Acts 17:13, 14) or it may have been related to the bond that the city authorities required Jason to post (Acts 17:9) that made him responsible to see that Paul "did not return to the city" (Marshall, *Acts*, p. 280). All we can say with certainty is that Satan's opposition was formidable enough to thwart Paul's best efforts to return. The devil down through history has done all he can to hinder evangelistic work and to sow discord between believers and their leaders. Such was the situation in Thessalonica.

On the other hand, the fact that Satan isn't all powerful is indicated by the fact that the apostle was eventually able to return to his churches in Macedonia (Acts 20:1-6; 1 Cor. 16:5). Thus God later opened the way in response to the prayer in 1 Thessalonians 3:11. One conclusion of the whole episode is that even though Satan is a formidable adversary, he is not an omnipotent one (see Dan. 10:12, 13 for a revealing behind-the-scenes look at the dynamics in the hindering efforts of the devil as he seeks to block the Lord's work).

In the meantime, God made something good come out of a difficult situation. After all, we wouldn't have Paul's letters to the Thessalonians if Paul had been able to return and meet with them in person. His letters became the substitute for his personal presence. Thus God managed to bless in spite of the apostle's difficulties. In the end, it is Satan who loses every battle with the divine Being to whom the apostle had devoted his life.

In 1 Thessalonians 2:19, 20 Paul brings his esteem for his converts to a climax. "You are our glory and joy," you are our "hope," "joy," and "crown of boasting." At first glance that seems to be a strange assertion for a person who found his hope in God alone and claimed that his only boasting was in the cross of Christ (Gal. 6:14).

Has Paul changed his mind? Not really. He still places his hope in the death and resurrection of Jesus (1 Thess. 4:13, 14), and his boasting is not in anything he has accomplished toward his salvation. Rather, as the context indicates, his hope in his converts is for the future, and his boasting will take place "in the presence of our Lord Jesus at His coming" when the apostle and his fellow missionaries are at last able to present their converts to Jesus as evidence of His grace in their ministry as revealed by the transformed lives of those whom they were able to bring the gospel message. What a joyful day that will be when we stand in Jesus' presence with those whom we have influenced for Him.

Meanwhile, with that future scene in view, we can join with Paul every day in seeing the renewed lives of those we have led to the kingdom as our joy, hope, and crown of boasting. Since we humans are going to boast about something, let it be in those who have given their lives to Jesus through God's use of our varied talents.

The best of news is that both those who sow and those who reap will stand together at the end of time "in the presence of our Lord Jesus." And with that thought we have come to the keynote for the rest of 1 Thessalonians. From this point on the letter looks ahead more and more to the Second Advent, when all the saved throughout the ages will meet their Lord at His return (see especially 4:13-17).

> ### Perspective on 1 Thessalonians 2:19, 20
>
> "What Paul seems to mean, in this transport of love, is that his joy in this world and his glory in the next are tied up with the Thessalonians, whom Christ through the apostle's ministry has so signally transformed" (Stott, p. 63).

9. Words of Concern and Timothy's Mission

1 Thessalonians 3:1-5

¹Therefore when we could endure it no longer, we determined to be left behind at Athens alone, ²and we sent Timothy our brother and God's co-worker in the gospel of Christ, to strengthen and encourage you in your faith, ³so that no one would be shaken by these afflictions. You yourselves know that we have been appointed to this. ⁴For even when we were with you, we kept telling you in advance that we were about to suffer affliction, and so it happened, as you know. ⁵For this reason, when I could endure it no longer, I also sent that I might know your faith, for fear that somehow the tempter might have tempted you, and our labor would be in vain.

Do you ever lie awake at night and worry about your children? It's hard not to at crucial junctures in their lives. We wonder if they are hanging around with the right people, going to church, staying healthy, and so on. The last thing we want is for them to go off the track. After all, we have loved them so much, sacrificed for them, and cared for them night and day throughout their growing up years. Has it all been for nothing?

Such were the emotions of Paul as he contemplated the fate of his "children in the Lord" in Thessalonica. He had more than once attempted to return to them for a visit, but had found himself blocked by Satan (1 Thess. 2:18). The longer his separation from the newly founded and only partially instructed congregation, the more he worried about them. Had Satan also thwarted their faith and led them away from the gospel? Given the aggressive nature of the Jewish community in Thessalonica and the troubles the new converts had begun to face about the time of his departure, he had genuine reasons for concern.

Paul, of course, was aware that Jesus said that Christians are not to be anxious about anything (Matt. 6:25-34). In fact, the apostle had taught the same thing (Phil. 4:6). And even now he undoubtedly recognized that there is a type of fearful, distrusting worry that is always wrong. But in situations in which people have responsibility for others, it is both natural and right to be concerned and even anxious about their well-being, especially if they can do something to help them.

When Paul and his fellow ministers could stand the tension no longer, they decided to send Timothy on a three-pronged mission to the newly established congregation (1 Thess. 3:2). Timothy's three goals were to

1. strengthen and encourage them in their faith (verse 2),

2. prevent them from being shaken out of their faith by the persecutions they were undergoing (verse 3), and

3. provide Paul with an update on their spiritual condition and needs (verse 5).

While Timothy may have been the junior member in the evangelistic team, he was well qualified for his task. And Paul wants the Thessalonians to understand that fact. Thus the apostle notes that Timothy is "our brother and God's coworker in the gospel of Christ" (verse 2). That commendation not only flagged Paul's personal confidence in the younger man, but was intended to send a clear message to the Thessalonians that the apostle valued them, so much so that he was willing to send a dedicated minister of proven talent to visit them.

Timothy's departure, unfortunately, was a sacrifice for Paul, who would be left alone in Athens, a city in which he had already been wearied by endless philosophical speculation and skepticism. While he hadn't been run out of town there as had been the case in Philippi, Thessalonica, and Berea, he had suffered the indignity of being largely ignored (Acts 17:16-34). Thus the last thing he needed emotionally was to be isolated at this low point in his ministry. But he was willing to undergo even more deprivation, since the tensions he had been feeling over the situation in Thessalonica had become unbearable.

Although Timothy's journey to Thessalonica would be his first independent mission, it wouldn't be his last. Paul would later send him on missions to Corinth (1 Cor. 4:17; 16:10, 11) and Philippi (Phil. 2:19-24). But such visits by the assistant evangelist could never substitute for those of the apostle himself. Paul repeatedly promised personal visits as a follow-up to his letters (1 Cor. 16:7; Phil. 2:24). That same pattern held true for the believers in Thessalonica. Even after Timothy's successful journey, Paul hoped to come personally, to "supply what is lacking" in their faith (1 Thess. 3:10, RSV). But since that was impossible at the time, he instead wrote the letter that we call 1 Thessalonians.

First Thessalonians 3:1-5 raises several theological issues. The first relates to the mission of Timothy to strengthen and encourage the believers in their faith. That commission, often summarized as a "ministry of follow-up," raises the question of the nature of the faith that needed to be strengthened. The Bible is rich in the nuances of Christian faith. One aspect is an individual's personal trust in God and the message of the gospel, what we can think of as saving faith. A second factor in faith is belief in the central facts of the Bible, such as the incarnation, death, and second coming of Jesus—the intellectual side of faith. The third aspect of faith is the experiential, continuing faithfulness to the God who has saved us through Jesus.

Which of those three, we might ask, does Timothy need to strengthen in the Thessalonians? Probably all of them, since the onslaught of persecution threatens people in every part of their lives and all the flavors of faith are interrelated in the human psyche and daily living. What threatens one segment of faith affects the whole.

A second issue concerns the question of whether people can really be "shaken" out of their faith by such afflictions as the Thessalonians were undergoing (1 Thess. 3:3) or, for that matter, by anything else. Here we have a rephrasing of the once-saved-always-saved argument that has divided Christians through the centuries, with one side advocating that it is impossible to fall from grace, and the other side pointing out that the Bible seems to teach that people

> **The Flavors of Faith**
>
> 1. The saving = trust in God for salvation
> 2. The intellectual = mental agreement with the Bible's teachings
> 3. The experiential = practicing the Bible's teachings in daily life (faithfulness)
>
> All three need encouragement and strengthening in our lives.

can lose faith and thus their salvation itself. Verse 3 definitely lines up with the latter perspective. Paul harbors no doubts that believers in the midst of persecution could be "'drawn aside,' 'allured' from the right path" (Milligan, p. 38). Verse 8, in which the apostle writes that they would be safe if they continued to "stand fast in the Lord" (RSV), reinforces that perspective. To not stand fast would be to be shaken out of faith itself, the very thing Paul fears in verse 3.

A third theological issue prominent in 1 Thessalonians 3:1-5 is what we might call a "theology of suffering" (Green, p. 162). After noting his concern that some believers might "be shaken by these afflictions" (verse 3a), Paul spends the next verse and a half in a "mini speech" on the topic of suffering and affliction in the Christian life. His first point is that such things are a part of a Christian's destiny. Jesus had earlier made that evident when He told His disciples that if people persecuted Him they would persecute them also (John 15:20) and that they would have tribulation in the world (John 16:33). And Paul, himself, would later comment that we should view such expected sufferings as occasions to rejoice, since they would develop Christian character (Rom. 5:3-5).

Dietrich Bonhoeffer in the midst of His death struggle with Hitler's Germany captured the essence of the theology of suffering when he wrote that "if we refuse to take up our cross and submit to suffering and rejection at the hands of men, we forfeit our fellowship with Christ and have ceased to follow him. But if we lose our lives in his service and carry our cross, we shall find our lives again in the fellowship of the cross of Christ. . . . To bear the cross proves to be the only way of triumphing over suffering. This is true for all who follow Christ, because it was true for him" (Bonhoeffer, p. 101).

Paul's next point in his theology of suffering in 1 Thessalonians 3:3, 4 is that they should not be surprised by persecution at the hands of their fellow Thessalonians. Rather, they should have expected it since he had pointed to the fact of Christ's suffering while he was with them (Acts 17:3) and had repeatedly told them that the same fate would happen to them (1 Thess. 3:4a). That prophecy had come true, as they very well knew, given their current situation.

Suffering raises a fourth theological concern in verse 5, in which the apostle introduces the topic of the role of the tempter and his activities in the lives of Christians. The tempter, of course, is Satan, who had hindered Paul from visiting the congregation (1 Thess. 2:18). Jesus had made that same equation in Matthew 4:3, 10. The temptation facing the Thessalonian congregation was not simply to commit some sin but rather to slip into apostasy. "All this trouble you are having," the tempter whispers in their ears, "surely can't be from God. You have obviously made a mistake," he continues, "but the good news is that things will go back to normal as soon as you drop these troublesome beliefs brought to you by that cowardly Paul, who fled in the night and has shown his lack of concern for you by not returning. Why not just quit and bring peace into your life?"

So goes the voice of the tempter—not only to the first-century Thessalonians, but also to those of us who live 20 centuries later. Satan would like nothing better than to discourage us and have us turn away from God's salvation in Christ.

It is against such an attack that Paul sent Timothy "to strengthen and encourage" the Thessalonians "in their faith." And he continues to dispatch "Timothys" in every generation. In fact, God is sending you and me today to be a Timothy to our struggling brothers and sisters in the faith. To every Christian He extends the ministry of encouragement. God wants me to be a Timothy to those suffering in my community.

10. Rejoicing Words: Good News From Timothy

1 Thessalonians 3:6-10

⁶But now that Timothy has come to us from you, and has brought us good news of your faith and love and that you always remember us kindly, longing to see us even as we also long to see you— ⁷for this reason, brothers, in all our distress and affliction we were comforted about you through your faith; ⁸for now we truly live, since you are standing firm in the Lord. ⁹For what thankfulness can we return to God concerning you for all the joy with which we rejoice in the presence of our God because of you, ¹⁰praying earnestly night and day that we might see your face and supply the deficiencies of your faith?

When intense frustration meets extreme joy the result is a profound emotional reaction. And that is what we find in 1 Thessalonians 3:6-10.

It had been a long wait for Paul. His fears had centered on the probability that his enemies in Thessalonica were seeking to undermine his character and teachings among the new believers, and, worse yet, that they might have rejected the faith he had risked so much to teach them. He had sent Timothy to them to strengthen and encourage them (verse 2) and to find out for the apostle if they were holding on in the midst of their persecution or whether they had caved in to the tempter (verse 5).

It had been a long month or so as Timothy journeyed from Athens to

Thessalonica, spent some time with the believers, and then returned to Paul, whose anxiety had not abated in the excruciating waiting period. In the meantime, the apostle had moved on to Corinth, which had its own problems that had further aggravated him. He described his condition at that time as being "in weakness and in much fear and trembling" (1 Cor. 2:3, RSV).

So much for our thoughts of the stoic apostle who could unflinchingly face all troubles in the stark courage of his faith. Such a vision of Paul places him in heaven rather than on earth. Wake up! Paul was one of us. Despite his apostolic calling, he was like us in his daily life. We need to abandon the concept that he was some type of super saint and catch the biblical view that he had the same struggles and temptations to discouragement that we have. And therein we find the importance of his example for our lives. His struggles provide us with a model as we move through the trials of life in the twenty-first century. We all want instant answers to our prayers, but such is not the usual course of life. It definitely wasn't for Paul as he struggled in Corinth while anxiously watching for Timothy's return.

Time may have dragged for the apostle, but Timothy did return, and with good news. At that point "the letter all but explodes with joy and thanks to God" (Green, p. 166). "But now . . . Timothy has come to us from you, and has brought us good news of your faith and love and that you always remember us kindly, longing to see us even as we also long to see you" (verse 6).

What better news could there be? Paul highlights three points:

1. The Thessalonian community was filled with "faith and love." In those two words, Reformer John Calvin asserts, Paul "comprehends briefly the entire sum of true piety" (Calvin, *Thessalonians*, p. 268). They were in the faith in the sense that they had maintained faith in Christ as Savior, they continued to believe the apostolic doctrines, and they had remained faithful in daily life in spite of their sufferings. That faith and faithfulness they daily exhibited in their lives of love.

2. The new congregation expressed kind thoughts about Paul and his associates. In other words, they had not been led astray by those who had been claiming that he didn't really care for them, as evidenced by his forsaking them to their sufferings after having fled when things heated up.

3. They desired to see Paul again. That was comforting news, compa-

rable to the situation of the modern parent who, for one reason or another, has had a distant or even broken relationship with a child for an extensive period of time, and then gets the joyful news that their loved one still cares and wants to set up a meeting. Joyful news for us. And so it was to Paul.

Two words in verse 6 literally jump off the page as we read them. The first is the verb associated with "good news" (*evangelizō* in the Greek), which means to bring good news or the gospel. "This is the only place in the N. T. where the verb . . . is used without a full and direct reference to the gospel which is Jesus Christ" (Best, p. 139). The very fact that Paul employs that profound word this one time in terms of something other than its connection with the preaching of salvation in Christ is a measure of the joy and relief that Timothy's message brought him.

The second word is the "now" of verse 6. Anxiety for his children in the faith may have clouded the past, but "now" the apostle is relieved. The "now" also indicates that he penned 1 Thessalonians soon after Timothy's arrival. He wastes no time addressing the Thessalonian church with a supercharged heart. In his letter he recalls his thanksgiving, struggles, and anxieties about the church in the *past* (1:1-3:5), but after his rebirth of hope in 3:6-13 he will turn in chapters 4 and 5 to the *present* concerns of the church expressed to him by Timothy. Thus the "now" of verse 6 indicates a temporal shift in the letter.

That brings us to the "now" of verse 8. Because of Timothy's good news, Paul felt truly alive again. All his anxiety had been washed away and it is as if he had been resurrected from the dead. At last he can move with confidence into the future. Or as George Milligan puts it, he had "a new lease on life" (Milligan, p. 40).

Part of that new energy bursts forth in prayer for the steadfast Thessalonians. The content of Paul's prayer appears in verses 11-13, while in verse 9 he describes the exuberant emotions undergirding that prayer.

"What thanksgiving is even possible over such good news" (Fee, p. 125). "Paul is overwhelmed with thankfulness to God, and there is no way to recompense God for all the joy with which he is rejoicing at the good news about their steadfastness" (Witherington, p. 96). His rhetorical question in verse 9 reminds us of the psalmist, who asked, "How can I repay the Lord for all his goodness to me?" (Ps. 116:12, NIV).

The answer is obvious. We can never repay God for His grace. All we can do is rejoice in His blessings, which exceed all bounds.

Verse 10 finds Paul moving from thanksgiving and joy to petition that he might soon be reunited with his Thessalonian children in the Lord. "Rather than [the] news satisfying Paul . . . , it has only intensified his desire to see his converts again" (Witherington, p. 96). The word *hyper-ekperissou*, which means "in over abundance, beyond all measure, superabundantly," "overflowing all bounds, exceedingly" (Mounce, p. 1298; Rogers, p. 477), captures the passion of Paul's prayer. The apostle is not halfhearted in prayer. He not only prays earnestly for the Thessalonians, but night and day, or constantly. Their needs never leave his mind. Here we find the core of his pastoral heart.

The content of his enthusiastic prayer of thanksgiving had two focal points. The first was that he might be able to see them again. Satan may have prevented him from returning thus far (1 Thess. 2:18), but he knew that the new believers required more than just letters to keep them on the right path. They needed the upbuilding that could come only from face-to-face encounters.

The second concern is that Paul could supply the deficiencies in their faith. As noted earlier, he and his team had been forced out of Thessalonica before they had fully instructed the new church in the Christian faith. As a result, the new believers had gaps both in their understanding and in their practice of Christian doctrine and living.

Paul will begin to supply those gaps or deficiencies in chapters 4 and 5, knowing full well that he can only begin the process in a letter—even one divinely inspired. The content of his instruction builds upon Timothy's report of the congregation's condition.

One line of instruction will focus on their deficient doctrinal understanding related to the Second Advent (1 Thess. 4:13-5:10), which the harried evangelists had not had time to clarify before their departure. A second line will deal with some teachings they had already received but not fully put into practice (1 Thess. 4:1-8) and some others that needed more emphasis (1 Thess. 4:9-12; 5:12-21).

First Thessalonians 4:1 turns to the instructional half of the letter. But before that Paul will offer a prayer for the Thessalonians in verses 11-13 of chapter 3.

11. Prayerful Words

1 Thessalonians 3:11-13

[11]Now may God Himself, even our Father, and our Lord Jesus direct our way to you; [12]and may the Lord cause you to increase and overflow in love to one another and to all people, just as we also do to you, [13]so that He may establish your hearts blameless in holiness before our God and Father at the coming of our Lord Jesus, with all His holy ones.

Paul has ended the long discussion of personal matters that dominated the first three chapters of 1 Thessalonians. His last statement was that he had been "praying earnestly" that he might see them face to face and instruct them further in the Christian faith (1 Thess. 3:10). In verse 11 he shifts from talking about praying to see them into an actual prayer: "Now may God Himself, even our Father, and our Lord Jesus Christ direct our way to you."

The first thing to note about that prayer is that Paul addresses it to both the Father and the Lord Jesus. G. K. Beale points out that "this conjunctive relationship between the Father and Christ and the fact that Paul's prayer is directed to both suggests strongly that Jesus shares the same divine status as the Father" (Beale, *1-2 Thessalonians*, p. 108). The prayer of 2 Thessalonians 2:16, which reverses the order and puts Jesus before the Father, reinforces the point.

In addition, we see the equality and unity of Jesus with the Father further highlighted by the fact that the two are the subject of the singular verb "direct." Even more significant is the petition in verse 12, addressed to Jesus alone ("Lord" is the name ascribed to Him in the New Testament). The fact that both verses 11 and 13 refer to Jesus as "Lord Jesus" also emphasizes His divinity, since *kurios* (Lord) was the name for God in the Greek translation of the Old Testament. Paul cements that identity through his citation of Zechariah 14:5 ("Then the Lord your God will come, and all the holy ones with him" [RSV]) in 1 Thessalonians 3:13, which identifies Jesus as God in that Old Testament passage. In that passage it is Jesus who comes "with all His holy ones."

The only conclusion that we can reach from Paul's prayer is that Jesus and the Father share divinity. Both together or either individually can answer our prayers. Thus we find the prayer to Jesus in verse 12 is an indicator of His divine power.

Leon Morris points out that in the prayer of 1 Thessalonians 3 we do not have "a formal trinitarian definition, but it is the kind of understanding of the nature of the Godhead that led inevitably to the formulation of the [doctrine] of the Trinity. This is all the more impressive in that it is done incidentally. Paul is not giving a theoretical discourse on the nature of deity, but engaging in prayer" (Morris, *First and Second*, 1991, p. 107). In other words, the apostle is not seeking to demonstrate the full deity of Jesus. Rather, his words flow out of and are built upon that doctrine. That is an important understanding since some claim that such a doctrine only came later in history as the church slid toward apostasy. Not so! The Thessalonian correspondence demonstrates that Paul believed in the full deity of Christ less than 20 years after His resurrection. He taught it without question as a foundation of the Christian faith.

At this juncture some ask where the Holy Spirit is, if this passage represents an essentially Trinitarian understanding. "The proper answer is that the [S]pirit is the one who is inspiring the prayer itself in Paul and his friends, and who is the hidden agency at work in the church to produce the results God and his people long to see. It is the [S]pirit who enables Christians to love one another, and those outside the church, with a love whose supply never dries up no matter what demands are made on it. It is the [S]pirit who settles the hearts of God's people to strive after holiness, to live without blame before God, and to become established and strengthened in that way of life. It is the [S]pirit who is at work in the present to prepare all God's people to be what he wants them to be when he appears again" (Wright, pp. 115, 116).

In short, the Spirit, like the Father and Jesus, is present all through the prayer. But that manifestation is not on the surface as it is with the first two members of the Godhead. And that lack of visible presence is quite in harmony with Jesus' teaching on the Holy Spirit when He said that the Spirit would bear witness to Jesus rather than to Himself (John 15:26). The Spirit has always been the least visible member of the Godhead.

Before we leave the addressees of Paul's prayer, we need to highlight two other points. The first is the personal touch represented in the twice repeated "our" when speaking to the Father and Jesus. We are not dealing with an impersonal God "way out there," but one who is accessible to each of us in a personal way.

The second point deals with the words "our Father," which hark back to Jesus' example prayer in Matthew 6:8. Here it is important to recognize that God is not Father to all people as many assume. While He is the creator of all people, the Bible plainly teaches that He is "our Father" to those born of the Holy Spirit (John 3:3, 5). The apostle John makes that teaching explicit when he writes that "to all who received him, who believed in his name, he gave power to become children of God; who were born, not of blood nor of the will of the flesh nor of the will of man, but of God" (John 1:12, 13, RSV; cf. Rom. 8:14-16; Gal. 4:5). In passing, we should note that "our Father" is not the only echo in Paul's prayer of Jesus' own model. Both prayers also point to doing God's will on earth and to the coming kingdom.

The Divine Jesus

"Paul is looking for Christ to do what no mere man could ever begin to do. None of the prayers to the Lord Jesus in these verses could possibly be answered in the slightest degree by a mere human being. . . . The deity of Christ is implicit all the way through the [Thessalonian] letters. It is not a controversy, but an essential cornerstone of the faith. If you want primitive Christology, here it is!" (Jackman, p. 85).

The prayer in 1 Thessalonians 3:11-13 has two petitions. The first is that the Father and the Lord Jesus would "direct" Paul and his associates back to Thessalonica. The Greek word I translated as "direct" can also be rendered as "clear the way" (NIV), "open the way" (REB), or "ease our path" (New Jerusalem). It alludes to making a straight path "by the leveling or removal of those obstacles with which Satan has obstructed it" (Lightfoot, p. 48). Thus the metaphor here relates directly to 1 Thessalonians 2:18, in which Paul states that "Satan hindered" his return to Thessalonica, utilizing a word for "hindered" that Greek also used when an army destroys a road "to block the way" of an invading force (Kittel, vol. 3, p. 855). First Thessalonians 3:11 reverses that blocking or hindering by straightening the way and clearing it so that Paul can return to his converts.

The good news about Paul's prayer is that it was eventually answered when he returned to Macedonia (Acts 20:1-3). The bad news is that his return took place about five years after he prayed so fervently. There is a lesson for us here. All too often we don't feel that our prayer has been answered or even heard unless we have immediate results. Paul's example should help us to see the larger picture. God is at work, but His answer to some of our prayers is "not yet."

The second petition was that the Lord would cause the love of the Thessalonians to "increase and overflow" to both fellow church members and to those in the larger community (1 Thess. 3:12). That was quite a prayer, when one realizes that the "all people" also included those persecuting them and bringing on their "suffering" (1 Thess. 2:14). But once again the apostle was echoing his Lord Jesus who had proclaimed, "Love your enemies and pray for those who persecute you" (Matt. 5:44, RSV). That is not an easy command in any age. But with the transforming power (Rom. 12:2) of the Holy Spirit and His empowerment in daily life it is possible for the born-again Christian.

In the petition to increase their love, Paul found a quicker fulfillment than in his first request. He repeatedly congratulated them on their fraternal love, not only for each other (1 Thess. 1:3; 4:9; 2 Thess. 1:3) but also for the churches throughout Macedonia (1 Thess. 4:9, 10). The apostle used them as a model for other Christian communities (2 Thess. 1:4). But even with their success, he encouraged them to grow in love "more and more" (1 Thess. 4:10, RSV).

With that love the Thessalonians had exhibited the very essence of what it means to be a Christian and to live God's law (see Matt. 22:34-40; Rom. 13:8-10; Gal. 5:14). Jesus reinforced that point when He proclaimed that "by this all men will know that you are my disciples, if you have love for one another" (John 13:35, RSV).

The prayer concludes with the reason for living the life of love in the present—that we might be "blameless in holiness before our God and Father at the coming of our Lord Jesus, with all His holy ones" (1 Thess. 3:13). "In order that we may be 'blameless and holy' then, Paul prays that we may be inwardly strengthened now" (Stott, p. 67). His concern for sanctified living in the present so that people will be ready for the return of Jesus is a theme that he continues to emphasize to the very end of 1 Thessalonians (see 1 Thess. 5:23).

The apostle's final focus in his prayer is that of being ready to meet Jesus when He comes "with all His holy ones" (verse 13). And who are those "holy ones"? That is an excellent question since many texts teach that both the angels and God's redeemed are His "holy ones" (see Malherbe, *Letters*, p. 214). And both may be included here. At least that is what Paul implies in 1 Thessalonians 4:13-17, which pictures Jesus' return to earth with His holy angels as His holy people are caught up to meet Him in the air.

With 1 Thessalonians 3:11-13 Paul has come to the end of his extended treatment of personal issues related to him and the Thessalonians. The next two chapters find him providing instruction on the Second Advent and living the Christian life, topics he has already prepared the way for in his short but insightful prayer.

Part III

Instructional Matters

1 Thessalonians 4:1-5:22

12. Instruction on Sexual Purity

1 Thessalonians 4:1-6a

> *¹Finally then, brothers, we request and exhort you in the Lord Jesus, that as you received instruction from us on how you ought to walk and to please God (as indeed you do walk), that you do so more and more. ²For you know what commands we gave you through the Lord Jesus. ³For this is the will of God, your sanctification: that you abstain from sexual immorality; ⁴that each one of you know how to control his own vessel in sanctification and honor, ⁵not in lustful passion like the Gentiles who do not know God; ⁶and that no one transgress and take advantage of his brother in this matter.*

First Thessalonians 4:1 is the pivot point between the two halves of the letter. The first three chapters find Paul reflecting on his evangelistic mission to Thessalonica and the events that followed. They include his defense of his actions and his anxiety over the new believers. The section climaxes with the return of Timothy, who reports that the church is doing very well. But Timothy also noted that its members had a few gaps in their knowledge and were not always practicing what they had been taught. Paul, therefore, desired to visit the new church so that he could further instruct them (1 Thess. 3:10). But since that was impossible at that time he decided to write them regarding their major needs in both the realms of ethical living and doctrinal understanding.

His first point of instruction takes up ethics, or how one ought to live day by day as a Christian—how they "ought to walk" so that they might "please God" (1 Thess. 4:1). Paul points out that he had already provided them with instruction along those lines and that they had already begun to live that way. But, he concludes in verse 1, they could do better.

Verse 2 finds the apostle describing that instruction as a "command" issued through the authority of the Lord Jesus. The word is forceful with military overtones, "denoting a 'word of command' received as from a superior officer that it may be passed on to others" (Milligan, p. 47). Here the order came by the authority of the Lord Jesus to Paul, who passed it on to his converts.

The heart of the command is that God's will was their "sanctification" (verse 3), a word that we can also translate as "holiness." The word *hagiasmos* appears again in verses 3 and 7, while 1 Thessalonians 5:23 contains its verbal form: "May the God of peace himself sanctify you wholly" (RSV). And 1 Thessalonians has already used a related word when Paul prayed that God would establish their hearts "blameless in holiness before our God and Father at the coming of our Lord Jesus, with all His holy ones" (1 Thess. 3:13).

It is significant that both 1 Thessalonians 5:23 and 3:13 emphasize holiness in the context of the Second Advent. That same connection occurs in the thrice-repeated desire for their holiness or sanctification in 1 Thessalonians 4:1-8, which immediately precedes a major discussion of the return of Jesus. Paul obviously wanted his converts to be ready for that event. Beyond that, from his discussion of the topic in 1 Thessalonians, he must have viewed the Second Advent as a motivating factor in their living a holy life. In that, the apostle was following Jesus in His admonition for His followers to "be ready" for His return (Matt. 24:44, 50; 25:10).

Before moving on, we need to spend more time understanding the meaning of sanctification or holiness. Holy or *hagios* is a basic term in this word group. It has the meaning of being "dedicated to God" (Bauer, pp. 10, 11). Thus the sanctuary and the priesthood were holy because they had been consecrated to Him. In a similar manner, the verb to sanctify (*hagiazō*) means to set something aside for holy use (*ibid.*, pp. 9, 10). When applied to Christians the word means that they "have been sanctified" (Acts 26:18; 1 Cor. 6:11; Heb. 10:14, note the past tense) or set apart for holy living. Thus the Christian's need for "sanctification" (1 Thess. 4:3).

Also close to the meaning of *hagios* or "holy" is the idea of different or "separate from common condition and use" or "dedicated" (Mounce, p.

1071). The very act of appointing something to holy use implies difference from the normal or being separated from something. For Christians that means being separated from the ways of the world and being dedicated to the ways and will of God.

It is unfortunate that too many people tune out of the very topic of holiness because they see it as a negative term focusing on what they can't do as Christians. While the word does have negative implications, as 1 Thessalonians 4:3-6 demonstrates, we should see the term primarily in a positive light. Holiness itself is rooted in the very character of God, who told the ancient Israelites, "Sanctify [consecrate, RSV] yourselves therefore, and be holy, for I am holy" (Lev. 11:44, NRSV). Peter indicates that that admonition applies to Christian believers when he wrote that "as he who called you is holy, be holy yourselves in all your conduct; since it is written, 'You shall be holy, for I am holy'" (1 Peter 1:15, 16, RSV). Thus in its essence holiness is a matter of becoming more and more like God.

In closing our discussion of holiness, it is "important to observe that God made the statement about holiness in Leviticus 11 to a people with whom he had already established a personal relationship. This means that the call to holiness is a call to discipleship, not a requirement for salvation.

> "One of the great weaknesses of contemporary evangelical Christianity is our comparative neglect of Christian ethics. . . . We are so busy preaching the gospel that we seldom teach the law. We are also afraid of being branded 'legalists.' 'We are not under the law,' we say piously, as if we were free to ignore and even disobey it. Whereas what Paul meant is that our acceptance before God is not due to our observance of the law. But Christians are still under obligation to keep God's moral law and commandments. . . . The purpose of the Holy Spirit's dwelling in our heart is that he might write God's law there" (Stott, p. 76).

Viewing holiness in this way helps us understand how Paul can view it as a future goal [1 Thess. 3:13] . . . , a past gift [1 Cor. 6:11], . . . and a journey [1 Thess. 4:3] to which God calls us (4:7)" (Holmes, p. 130).

In 1 Thessalonians 4:1-6, Paul may have started out by talking about the general principle of sanctification, but in the last half of verse 3 he raises a point that Timothy undoubtedly had reported to him after his return from his visit to Thessalonica: that the Thessalonians were having trouble with "sexual immorality."

It was no accident that the apostle focused on that topic for his initial piece of advice for two reasons. First, sexual morality in the Greco-Roman world was about as low as it could get. Prostitution was legal and was often a part of pagan worship, "pederasty was also widely practiced and was considered an acceptable form of sexual expression between an adult male and a prepubescent teen," and even the pagan gods got into the act with Zeus' (ruler of the gods) affairs with women and boys providing a model for both the other gods and the people of that day (Hubbard, pp. 187, 188).

The second reason that sexuality was a timely topic for the Thessalonians is that they had recently come into the Christian faith from that sexually immoral culture. Beyond that, "they were still in the midst of such a society and the infection of it was playing upon them all the time. It would be exceedingly difficult for them to unlearn what they had for all their lives accepted as natural" (Barclay, p. 230).

With those realities facing the recently converted Thessalonians, Paul reinforces two "commands" that he had previously given them. On the one hand was the negative: "abstain from sexual immorality" (1 Thess. 4:3) and the "lustful passions" of the surrounding culture (verse 5). Here the apostle used the Greek word *porneia* (from which we derive pornography), which means "unlawful sexual intercourse, prostitution, unchastity, fornication" (Bauer, p. 854) both inside and outside of a marriage relationship.

But the apostle didn't stop with the negative in his discussion of sex. He went on in verse 4 to say that each of his readers needed to "know how to control his own vessel in sanctification and honor." Here is the Bible's good news about sex—a teaching too often neglected in Christian teaching. Roy Stedman reflects upon that omission, writing that "when I was a young man, nobody was teaching about sexuality. Back then, you grew up thinking that your body ended at the waist" (Stedman, p. 59).

That is not the Bible picture. Genesis 1:26, 27 states that God made both males and females, Genesis 1:26, 27; 2:24 defines marriage as being between a male and a female, and Jesus made that combination foundational to sexual ethics in Christianity when He asserted that "a man shall leave his father and mother and be joined to his wife [the male and female of Gen. 2:24], and the two [not three or six] shall become one flesh" (Matt. 19:5, RSV). The Old Testament is so excited about the positive side of sex that it devotes an entire book to the topic—the Song of Solomon (Knight, *Song*, pp. 151, 152, 154-157).

We should note that there is a serious question as to whether 1 Thessalonians 4:4 should read "control his own vessel [body]" or "possess his own wife." But no matter which is the correct reading, the point is that Christians need to be holy and honorable in the realm of sex and different from the standards set by society and today's media. That includes taking advantage of another person for one's own sexual gratification (1 Thess. 4:6).

It has been rightly claimed that one of the greatest contributions of Christianity to the world is its revolutionary ideas regarding sexual purity and wholesomeness. And that contribution went far in the Christian world toward forming proper ideas on the topic. But we now live in what we can call the post-Christian era—a time in which the loose morality portrayed in television and other media provides the culture's understanding of sexual rights and wrongs. And with that change of models, the postmodern world has reverted largely to the Greco-Roman sexual morality in which almost anything goes between individuals of both sexes.

As a result, Paul's teaching on the topic is as relevant today as it was 2,000 years ago. We as Christians need to be honorable and holy in this realm, and the church must be vocal in standing for Bible principles on this important topic. Not to do so means that the Christians lose and the Greeks win. That very possibility concerned Paul as he fretted over his beautiful congregation in Thessalonica.

13. Instruction Regarding the Seriousness of God

1 Thessalonians 4:6b-8

⁶ᵇbecause the Lord is the avenger concerning all these things, even as we also told you before and solemnly warned you. ⁷For God has not called us for impurity, but in sanctification. ⁸Therefore the one who rejects this is not rejecting man but the God who gives His Holy Spirit to you.

The perceptive reader has noted that I began this portion of scripture in mid-sentence, signaled by "because" with a lower case "b." The "because" refers to 1 Thessalonians 4:1-6a, which deal with the Thessalonian church members' (or at least some of them) ongoing difficulty living a sexually moral life in the midst of a culture (like today's) in which sexual immorality was a central feature of life, often even as a part of worship of their pagan gods.

The "because" is important since it signals the message that all forms of *porneia* or "sexual immorality" (verse 3) have serious consequences. But before we get to them, we need to look at another word that joins 1 Thessalonians 6b-8 to the first half of the paragraph. That word is "sanctification" or "holiness," found in verses 3 and 7. The point that we must make here is that 1 Thessalonians repeatedly links holy or sanctified living with the Second Advent (1 Thess. 3:13; 5:23), the very time at which, Jesus tells us, people will reap the results of their lives here on earth (Matt. 16:27; Rev. 22:12).

In other words, no matter how people conduct their lives, there will be consequences, a teaching that both Paul and Jesus present elsewhere (e.g. Rom. 6:12-23; Matt. 7:13, 14). Within that general context, 1 Thessalonians 4 will conclude with the results of holiness at the Second Advent in verses 13-18, in which Paul presents a description of the resurrection and/or ascension of the righteous to meet Jesus on the final day of reckoning. By way of contrast, 1 Thessalonians 6b alludes to the fate of the wicked when it refers to the Lord as "the avenger" of those who reject His ways (verse 8) and continue to live in immorality. The word "avenger" is an interesting one, especially since it implies that Jesus as "Lord" will be the agent of that avenging. That puts Him in the same role as does the book of Revelation, which speaks of the "wrath of the Lamb" (Rev. 6:16).

The word translated as "avenger" (*ekdikos*) means "one who carries out that which is right" (Rogers, p. 478), and thus it refers to "the man who carries out a sentence" (Moulton, p. 193) or "one who punishes" (Bauer, p. 301). Romans 12:19, which quotes God as saying "vengeance is mine, I will repay, says the Lord" (RSV), employs a related word. In terms of the avenger in 1 Thessalonians 4:6, Charles Wanamaker suggests that Paul "probably has in mind here an apocalyptic image of the Lord Jesus as the coming avenger or agent of God's wrath who will inflict severe punishment on wrongdoers who violate the demands of the gospel. This understanding fits with the sense of imminent expectation and the apocalyptic imagery found in 1 and 2 Thessalonians (cf. 1:10; 5:1-11; 2 Thess. 1:7-10)" (Wanamaker, p. 156).

The word "avenger," as Wanamaker has indicated, is closely tied to the term "wrath" (*orgē*), which 1 Thessalonians uses three times, each in an eschatological context (1 Thess. 1:10; 2:16; 5:9). Second Thessalonians 1:7-9 puts the parts of the picture together when Paul speaks of the time "when the Lord Jesus is revealed from heaven with his mighty angels in flaming fire, inflicting vengeance upon those who do not know God and upon those who do not obey the gospel of our Lord Jesus. They shall suffer the punishment of eternal destruction and exclusion from the presence of the Lord and from the glory of his might" (RSV).

Such is the teaching of the Thessalonian letters harbored in the word "avenger" in 1 Thessalonians 4:6. Of course, we need to ask why that theme plays such a prominent and consistent role in Paul's two epistles. The only possible answer is that it was an important topic that he definitely wanted his readers to understand. In short, his repeated emphasis tells his readers that sin (sexual and otherwise) is not something to treat lightly, that God will eventually make things right when Jesus comes.

Now the topic of God's wrath or His being an "avenger" has not been very popular with "well educated" and "sophisticated" modern Christians. But the sophisticated didn't regard it with favor in Paul's day either. On the other hand, the theme of wrath was very popular with God. The number of Bible references to divine wrath exceeds 580. But on this topic we need to be careful. God's wrath is not an emotional anger comparable with human wrath. To the contrary, His wrath is a function of His love. God hates the sin that continues to destroy the lives of His created beings. He is weary of dead babies, exploited lives, cancer, and racial holocausts.

In His own timing God will respond to the problem of sin and make things right and put an end to the destruction brought about by irresponsible living. W. L. Walker points out that God's "wrath only goes forth because God is love, and because sin is that which injures His children and is opposed to the purpose of His love" (Walker, pp. 148, 149). And Alan Richardson notes that "only a certain kind of degenerate Protestant theology has attempted to contrast the wrath of God with the mercy of Christ" (Richardson, p. 77).

In summary, God's wrath and its related avenging of 1 Thessalonians 4:6 is a part of the good news that we call the gospel. "God, as the Bible pictures Him, cannot and will not stand idly by while His creation suffers. *His reaction is judgment on sin, and we should see this judgment as the real meaning of biblical wrath.* God condemns sin in judgment and will eventually move to destroy it completely" (Knight, *Cross*, p. 39). That teaching is central to both of the letters to Thessalonica.

Thus Paul's use of "avenger" in 1 Thessalonians 4:6 is a wake-up call to those who had been disregarding his teachings on Christian morality, especially the sexual immorality he discussed in chapter 4. It is also a reminder to us who live in a culture that does not want to hear such talk.

But the church today needs to hear such warnings, for it has all too often forgotten the same thing that some of the Thessalonians had. Namely, that sexual activity outside of a biblical marriage relationship is not merely an activity between two "consenting adults" for their mutual pleasure but a sin against God and other people and thus the antithesis of that love that Jesus claimed was the foundation of God's law (Matt. 22:36-40).

The modern approach to the topic that fueled the "sexual revolution" of the 1960s and beyond roots itself in psychological and cultural reasons for what the Bible refers to as "sexual immorality." But Paul returns the frame of reference for the argument back to the theological. As a result, Beverly Gaventa proposes that "teachers and preachers might . . . explore the question: What does it mean to engage in sexual intercourse 'in holiness and honor'? [1 Thess. 4:4]" (Gaventa, p. 56). And Michael Holmes asserts that the church must "reconsider some of the distinctions it makes between various categories of sex-

> **What We Moderns Do Not Want to Hear**
>
> "Paul uses the ultimate sanction—the Lord Jesus is a punisher of all such sins. We live in a culture that does not want to hear that. It wants to hear that the Lord Jesus understands my temptations and condones my sins. But Paul says the Lord Jesus is a punisher of all such sins. The will of God [is] for our sanctification" (Jackman, p. 102).

ual misbehavior. For Paul, whether sexual immorality occurred in an oppo-site-sex or same-sex context was essentially insignificant (cf. 1 Cor. 6:9-10, 'neither the sexually immoral . . . nor adulterers nor male prostitutes nor ho-mosexual offenders . . . will inherit the kingdom of God'). . . . Many denom-inations or segments of the church have lost their ability and authority to speak clearly on sexual matters. . . . Paul's instructions to the Thessalonians offer a biblical antidote to our current confusion" (Holmes, p. 134).

First Thessalonians 4:7 returns to the sexual issues of verses 1-6a by stating that God did not call Christians so that they could remain sexually impure, but so that they could be sanctified or set apart from the world in sexual matters. Being a realist, the apostle recognized that his teaching on the topic would not win any popularity contests. As a result, he closes off the topic by stating that "the one who rejects this is not rejecting man but the God who gives His Holy Spirit to you" (verse 8).

Verse 8 contains several things that we should note. The first is that the apostle rams home the truth that the teachings of sexual conduct he has set forth are those of God rather than of any person, including himself. Apparently some were claiming that Paul's proclamations on sexual moral-ity were merely his opinion on the topic and thus not authoritative. "Such people would have distinguished between the gospel proclamation, which they received as divine (2:13), and the moral teaching on sexuality, which they rejected as coming simply from a man" (Green, p. 200). Not so, the apostle states. The teaching has the authority of God behind it, and, there-fore, whoever "rejects this is not rejecting man but the God who gives His Holy Spirit to you" (1 Thess. 4:8).

That thought brings us to the Holy Spirit, whom the Greek text iden-tifies in an unusual way as "His Spirit, the holy." That word order, which emphasizes the holiness of the Spirit, stands in stark contrast to the unho-liness or "impurity" (verse 7) of those going against Paul's teaching on the topic. Verse 8 also implies that if they persist in rejecting the apostle's teaching on the topic they will be continuing to spurn the Holy Spirit, which Jesus defined as the one unpardonable sin (Matt. 12:31).

Serious indeed are our attitudes and actions in the light of God's rev-elation to the apostles that have been preserved for us in the New Testament. Its teachings, including those on morality, are not merely good advice but God's Word to us.

14. Instruction on Love and Labor

1 Thessalonians 4:9-12

⁹Now concerning brotherly love, you have no need for me to write to you, for you yourselves are taught of God to love one another; ¹⁰for indeed you do it to all the brothers throughout Macedonia. But we exhort you, brothers, to excel even more, ¹¹and to be ambitious to live quietly and to mind your own business and to work with your own hands, even as we commanded you; ¹²so that you may live in a becoming manner among outsiders and have need of nothing.

This passage begins with praise but ends in warning. It starts with love and concludes with work. At first glance those seem to be strange combinations. But read in its totality and within the larger context of Thessalonians, the paragraph has a logic to it.

We need to note two aspects of that context. First, just as 1 Thessalonians 4:1-8 is a response to Paul's prayer in 3:13 regarding their living a life of holiness, so 4:9-12 is a response to 3:12 in which Paul prayed that the Lord might cause them "to increase and overflow in love to one another and to all people." The second crucial contextual aspect is a concern with the eminence of the Second Advent, which Paul treats in 1 Thessalonians 4:13-5:10. Given those backgrounds, we can summarize the message of 1 Thessalonians 4:9-12 as "how to live a life of love in the face of the pending advent."

Another thing to note about our passage is that it begins with "now concerning." That same phrase appears in the lead sentences to Paul's next two paragraphs (in 5:1 exactly as in 4:9, and in 4:13 with some variation). He uses the same phrase in 1 Corinthians 7:1, in which he writes, "now concerning the matters about which you wrote" (RSV). What we have here is a list of questions raised by the Thessalonians that Timothy had brought back with him in either oral or written form from his recent visit to Thessalonica. Whereas in verses 1-8 Paul raised his own concern with Timothy's report over the moral laxity of some of the new believers, beginning in verse 9 he will begin to address what worried them.

The central problem in verses 9-12 does not seem to be that of love itself, but how to live lovingly in the face of what the Thessalonians believed to be a Second Coming that would take place very soon. From a contextual reading of verses 9-12 it appears that in their newfound faith the church members had become emotionally excited in the face of what they believed would be the imminent return of Christ. The result had been that many of them had given up their daily work and "were standing about in excited groups, upsetting themselves and everybody else, while they waited for the Second Coming to arrive. Ordinary life had been disrupted" and "the problem of making a living had been abandoned" (Barclay, p. 233). The new believers were wondering what to do about the situation. Paul's response is one of practicality as he replies on two levels: a general principle (verses 9 and 10) and specific counsels (verses 11 and 12). The counsel itself has been helpful down through the ages as various groups have become overly emotional about the return of Jesus, leading to situations similar to that found in verses 9-12.

Beginning with the general principle that ought to guide all Christian living, in verse 9 Paul raises the issue of love. Speaking to the "brotherly love" of those within the Christian community, he has many good things to say about the Thessalonian converts. On the other hand, as we will see in verse 12, he believes that some of them are falling short in their witness of love to the non-Christians in the larger society.

"Concerning brotherly love, you have no need for me to write to you." Here we have a rhetorical convention by which the apostle first confirms his readers in what they are doing right, which becomes a foundation for emphasizing the need for more of the same and to develop it even further. But we have more than a rhetorical technique. Paul is quite genuine in his praise of their love for others in their Christian community. Repeatedly throughout the Thessalonian correspondence he commends believers for their mutual love for one another (1 Thess. 1:3; 3:6, 12; 5:8, 13; 2 Thess. 1:3; 3:5). James Denney writes that "the early Christian churches were little companies of people where love was at a high temperature, where outward pressure very often tightened the inward bonds, and where mutual confidence diffused continual joy" (Denney, p. 154). That picture certainly seems to be true for the church in Thessalonica. But it wasn't free from problems in that line, as possibly evidenced by the allusion to some of them wronging others through sexual immorality (1 Thess.

4:6). Whatever the situation might have been, Paul urged them to improve ("excel even more") in their love even to other Christians.

So far so good for the paragraph running from verses 9 through 12. But with verse 11 he begins to deal with certain problems troubling the Christian community in Thessalonica. He raises three issues. First, their need to desire "to live quietly." The apostle actually makes it stronger. His wording suggests that they need "to be ambitious" to achieve that goal, which implies that reaching it may take some effort on their part. Such an appeal leads us to wonder what the problem was. We find a partial answer in his second and third admonitions, but the wording in the phrase itself "is an appeal to them not to let their enthusiasm" about the Second Advent "get the better of them" so that they lived on the edge of perpetual excitement that kept both themselves and others in the church in a state of restlessness (Neil, *Thessalonians*, pp. 86, 87).

Paul's second imperative is for them to mind their own business. Here we find both a problem and a cure for the ceaseless excitement addressed in his first command. Minding their own business might mean one of two things. One is that they may have been playing the part of busybodies. That was certainly a problem among the nonworking segment of the congregation in 2 Thessalonians 3:11. Not having enough to do, they were not only unnaturally agitated but also were gossiping and falling into mischief, including perhaps the moral issue dealt with in 1 Thessalonians 4:1-8.

But there is a second possible meaning—namely, to get on with the business of life rather than suspending activity until the eschaton. William Neil tells the story of a later time when excitement was running high concerning the nearness of the end of the world. When a sudden darkness enveloped the legislative session of the assembly, "some cried fearfully: 'It is the coming of Christ: it is the end of the world.' But the old President ordered lights to be produced: 'bring in candles,' he said, 'and get on with your work. If the Lord is coming, how better can He find us than quietly doing our duty" (Neil, *Thessalonians*, p. 87). Should Paul have had that meaning in mind, he would have been reinforcing the teaching of Jesus, who taught that not only should people watch and be ready for His return, but that they should be doing their duty up till that event (see Matt. 24:36-25:46). The alternative is to fritter away one's time in endless excitement that might keep everyone stirred up but produces no good for either other people or God's kingdom. A problematic issue among many of those who believe in a soon coming Jesus is that it is easier for them to focus on time and excitement related to nearness rather than being faithful stewards and living as responsible Christians in the interim. That was a problem in Paul's day, it has been so down through history in times of eschatological tumult, and it is still an issue in our time.

Paul's third imperative for the waiting Thessalonians is for them to work with their hands, as he had earlier commanded them. As noted previously, the word "command" is a strong verb of military force. Undoubtedly Paul needed to use such a forceful term in a world that regarded working with one's hands with disfavor. Furthermore, why work, the logic runs, if Jesus is soon to return and the things of this world will be of no value? Why not just rejoice in our new faith as we await the Lord's coming? That must have been a genuine temptation to those who belonged to the looked-down-upon lower, laboring class and to those who were slaves, as were many of the early Christians.

But what was its impact on the larger community? That is the issue that Paul addresses in 1 Thessalonians 4:12, in which he writes that they needed to work with their hands "so that you may live in a becoming manner." Or, as the Revised Standard Version renders the passage: "so that you may command the respect of outsiders." If Christians are known by the fruit of their lives (Matt. 7:15-20), what a false impression they give to the non-Christian community if believers quit working and sponge off of others who either have more or are still productive. Such a state of affairs would tend to turn many away from the Christian message as being socially and economically irresponsible. It was hardly an act of love to the larger community. Thus even though Paul could commend the Thessalonians for their love to one another, he definitely believed that they could portray a more loving picture to those around them.

Before he closes the topic, the apostle presents three reasons why Christians should be faithful in useful work: (1) it will keep them out of the mischief he discussed in verse 11, (2) it will improve their reputation in the nonchurched community, and (3) it will take care of their necessities. Such reasons are still important and needed in the twenty-first century. God has given talents to each of us, and He has appointed each of us a task or tasks to do until He arrives in the clouds of heaven. When He returns, He will declare that those who have been faithful in the common things of life are ready to enter His kingdom (Matt. 24:45-25:46). As a result, Paul's words and instruction in 1 Thessalonians will continue to have great value for each of us as we await that Day.

15. Instruction on Death: Introducing the "Blessed Hope"

1 Thessalonians 4:13

¹³Now we do not want you to be ignorant, brothers, concerning those sleeping, so that you will not grieve as others who have no hope.

We have come to the second "now . . . concerning," which signals that Paul is addressing the second issue in the list of questions brought back by Timothy that the Thessalonian members wanted answered. This one deals with the meaning of death for Christians. More specifically, what will happen "to the dead in Christ"? (1 Thess. 4:16).

It had been only a short time since Paul had established the church in Thessalonica, but already some of them had died. That had apparently caught the new believers by surprise. With their expectation that Christ would return very soon (see 2 Thess. 2:2, 3), they may have assumed that all believers would live until the Second Advent. But some hadn't made it, and the Thessalonian church members had the sorrowful task of burying them. What would become of such individuals? Had they died because of some sin that they were being punished for? Had they lost their eternal reward? While we don't know the exact situation, the above sketch represents in a general way the problematic issue they were wrestling with—an issue that they may have even been arguing over. Thus their need for an answer from the apostle himself.

Here, I might add, is a problem that troubles people in every generation. After all, none of us escapes death. It is a fact of everyday existence. All those living will eventually die. So what is the meaning of death, or even of a life destined to end in such a useless manner? Here is a question that has challenged philosophers, theologians, and ordinary people across the ages. Paul's answer is the most satisfactory ever given.

The problem with the passage running from verses 13 to 18 is not uncertainty about the situation behind it, but, rather, why didn't the church understand such a basic issue? Commentators have proposed several answers. A first is that Paul had neglected to teach the Thessalonians about the resurrection of the dead. That suggestion is very difficult to maintain. After all, they knew that Christ had died and resurrected, a teaching that the apostle had taught them in his initial work in Thessalonica (Acts 17:3). Beyond that, Paul himself had been a Pharisee and thus a firm believer on the resurrection of the dead. And after he became a Christian he saw clearly that the resurrection of Christ is directly related to that of believers (1 Cor. 15:20-23). Given those facts, it is highly unlikely that the apostle did not present the topic of the resurrection of the dead to the new Christians in Thessalonica.

Other proposals speculate that a false doctrine had infiltrated the church that had led to doubt regarding the resurrection of the dead and/or even the second coming of Jesus. But neither idea finds support in the text, which pictures the author clarifying basic understanding rather than defending such beliefs.

Gene Green offers a more likely explanation, proposing that "the Thessalonians had received instruction about the resurrection but in the moment of confronting the reality of death became consumed with grief" (Green, p. 214). That is, they understand the doctrine intellectually, but the shock of the emotional reality of death blurred their application of what they knew to what they felt. Such a situation is familiar to anyone who has had to deal with the overwhelming impact of a sudden crisis. Disorienting is the only way to describe the reaction.

That last explanation, coupled with the possibility that they may not have understood the full reality of the doctrine of the resurrection of the dead, supplies us with the most likely explanation as to why Paul had to set forth the teachings of verses 13-18. What is quite clear from 1 Thessalonians is that the believers were experiencing grief and confusion because of the death of some of their members, and that he is responding out of a deep pastoral concern.

Pastor Paul writes that he does not want them to be ignorant about those who were sleeping (verse 13a). The word I translated as "ignorant" literally means "no knowledge." The apostle's antidote is to supply them with adequate Christian information on the topic.

"Sleeping" is an interesting word widely used in the Bible to refer to death. Thus Daniel writes that "many of those who sleep in the dust of the earth shall awake, some to everlasting life, and some to shame and everlasting contempt" (Dan. 12:4, RSV). And Jesus could say that "Lazarus has fallen asleep" and then explain His full meaning by noting that "Lazarus is dead" (John 11:11-14). It is of more than passing interest that both of those passages refer to the sleep of death in the context of resurrection. Paul is building upon a well-established biblical pattern.

Christians, verse 13 continues, do not need to "grieve as others who have no hope." It is important to recognize that the apostle is not saying that believers should not grieve, but that they should not do so like those who have no hope. Mourning is natural and emotionally necessary when we lose a loved one. Augustine of Hippo (A.D. 354-430) points out that "Paul didn't just say that you may not be saddened, but that you may not be saddened as the heathen are, who do not have any hope. It is unavoidable, after all, that you should be saddened; but when you feel sad, let hope console you" (Augustine in *Gorday*, p. 85).

The apostle describes non-Christians as having "no hope" in verse 13. Ernest Best suggests that "it is wrong to say that 'the rest of men' had no hope whatsoever. Many philosophers had taught that the soul was immortal, . . . but philosophic teaching had hardly penetrated to the common people" (Best, p. 185). But even the philosopher's hope of immortality was based upon speculation rather than certainty. Thus, in the eyes of Paul, it was "no hope" at all. The Greek poet Theocritus (3rd c. B.C.) reflects on the absence of hope when he writes that "hopes are for the living; the dead are without hope." Again a second-century mourner wrote, "I wept for Didymas. . . . But nevertheless, against such things one can do nothing. Therefore comfort ye one another" (both quotations are in Green, pp. 218, 219).

> "What Paul prohibits is not grief but hopeless grief" (Stott, p. 94).

But Paul would say that such comfort is no comfort at all, that such hope is no hope at all. It is only Christianity that supplies what he calls "our blessed hope" (Titus 2:13), defined in 1 Thessalonians 4:14-17 as the resurrection of the dead at Christ's second coming.

Instruction on Death: Introducing the "Blessed Hope"

It was into a world hopeless in the face of death that Paul proclaimed his gospel of hope. And hope itself was the essence of that good news. In his letter to the Romans, Paul refers to God as the "God of hope" (15:13) and notes that Christians "rejoice in our hope of sharing the glory of God" (5:2, RSV). I should point out that "hope" in the New Testament does not mean "wishful thinking," in the sense that I hope something might happen. "Quite to the contrary, 'hope' in the NT connotes 'a confident expectation,'" as in I know something *will* happen. "The confidence of Christian hope derives from the fact that God can be counted on to fulfill what yet remains to be accomplished for the church" (Harrison, p. 216). And confidence regarding about what God will do in the future rests upon what He has already done in the past. Therefore, Paul writes, "whatever was written in former days was written for our instruction, that by steadfastness and by the encouragement of the scriptures we might have hope" (Rom. 15:4, RSV).

And at the heart of hope in 1 Thessalonians 4:13-18 is the second coming of Jesus and the resurrection of believers, at which time the cry will be:

"Death is swallowed up in victory.
O death, where is thy victory?
O death, where is thy sting?"

The Missing Ingredient in Non-Christian Grief

The Greek world had its own ways of handling grief. The most common were:

"1. Death is inevitable," so why worry about that which cannot be helped.

"2. Death is the fate of all, kings and beggars, rich and poor," so you are no worse off than others.

"3. The person's memory and honor will live on in spite of death."

"4. Death releases one from the evils of life," so we ought to be thankful for it.

"5. The funeral and the tomb are a great honor to the deceased."

"6. Either death is nonexistence and does not matter to the dead or it leads to some happier state of existence," but there was no certain knowledge what that state might be. It was speculation at best (Stowers, p. 142).

Into that uncertain world Paul brought the only true hope in the face of grief—the Second Advent and the resurrection of the faithful dead.

(1 Cor. 15:54, 55, RSV).

That victory stands in ultimate contrast to those who are without hope in the face of death (1 Thess. 4:13). No wonder Paul refers to the Second Advent as the "blessed hope" (Titus 2:13).

16. Instruction on Death: Introducing the Resurrection

1 Thessalonians 4:14

¹⁴For since we believe that Jesus died and rose, even so God will take with Him those who have fallen asleep in Jesus.

The "for" at the head of verse 14 refers us back to verse 13, which noted that Christians are not like those who have no hope in the face of death. Why? "For," or because, "we believe that Jesus died and rose" and that "God will take with Him those who have fallen asleep in Jesus." Thus Paul built the Christian case for hope on two propositions:

1. Jesus died and rose, and

2. because He rose, those who have accepted Him will rise also.

The resurrection of Jesus was no new topic for the Thessalonians. Acts 17:3 tells us that Paul had explained and proved to them during his evangelistic campaign in Thessalonica "that it was necessary for the Christ to suffer and to rise from the dead" (RSV). Beyond that, 1 Thessalonians 1:10 indicates that the new believers must have accepted that teaching, since they were waiting for the return of Jesus from heaven, who had been resurrected from the dead.

For Paul, the very center of his definition of the gospel was that "Christ died for our sins in accordance with the scriptures, that he was buried, that he was raised on the third day" (1 Cor. 15:1, 3, 4, RSV). Or as L. J. Kreitzer nicely summarizes it: "The resurrection of Jesus Christ stands as the central motif in Paul's eschatology insofar as it inaugurates the age to come and provides the basis for future hope" (Kreitzer, in Hawthorne, p. 806).

That thought brings us to the word "since" in 1 Thessalonians 4:14.

The idea is that Christians have hope in death because (since) Jesus rose from the dead. "The resurrection of Christ and the resurrection of the faithful on the last day are related, the hope of the latter being based upon the certainty of the former" (*ibid.*). In short, because He has been raised, his followers will rise also. That thought is set forth in Revelation 1:17, 18, in which Jesus tells His followers: "Do not be afraid; I am the first and the last, and the living One; and I was dead, and behold, I am alive forevermore, and I have the keys of death and of Hades" or the grave (NASB). Thus it is that "since" Christians believe in Jesus they can be certain of their own resurrection from the dead. It is little wonder that Paul plants believers in the realm of the hopeful (literally those *full of hope*) as opposed to those who are hopeless (1 Thess. 4:13).

Verse 14 tells us that "God will take with Him those who have fallen asleep in Jesus." Several issues jump out in that short saying. The first is whether the correct translation should be those who fall asleep "in" Jesus, or as many versions have it, "through Jesus." That is an important question, since the word I translated as "in" generally translates as "through." But it doesn't make sense to say that people die through Jesus, since Jesus is always, according to Paul, the enemy of death (1 Cor. 15:26). As a result, "those who have fallen asleep in Jesus" is the better translation, since it is that group whom Paul pictures as being resurrected to meet Him in the air in verses 16, 17. Of course, "through" could be attached to the verb "take," which would indicate that believers are resurrected "through what Jesus has done" (Morris, *First and Second*, 1991, p. 139). The good news is that both statements are true, and when put together they make a powerful gospel statement: it is those who have died in relationship to Jesus who will be resurrected through His power over death.

That thought brings us to the word "take." Here we have another issue of importance, since the Greek word can imply either "bring" or "take." "The meaning of the word translated as *will take back* varies according to the context" (Ellingworth, p. 97). In verse 14 it has two possible meanings: either Jesus will bring from heaven those who supposedly went there at death, or Jesus will take to heaven those whom He resurrects at the Second Advent. Verse 16 settles the issue because it "fills out the meaning of verse 14" with its discussion of the resurrection of those who have died believing in Christ (*ibid.*). It is that group that Jesus will "*take*" to heaven when He comes as they are "caught up . . . in the clouds to meet with the Lord in the air" (verse 17).

"But," some might ask, "are you really certain that Jesus won't bring them back from heaven when He returns again? After all, didn't their immortal souls go to Jesus when they died? Isn't that what Paul taught when he suggested that to die was 'to depart and be with Christ' (Phil. 1:23, RSV)? Isn't that a clear teaching that Paul believed that his spirit or soul would return to God at death?"

Those are important questions. The first thing that we should point out is that the Bible does not teach that humans have immortal souls. To the contrary, it clearly spells out that God alone is immortal (1 Tim. 6:16). On the other hand, it also indicates that He will give immortality to human beings, but only to those who have accepted Christ, and only then at the second coming of Jesus (1 Cor. 15:51-55). As a result, it is impossible for a Christian's immortal soul to return to heaven at death because they do not yet have one.

On the other hand, believers already have what Jesus calls "eternal life" (John 3:36; 5:24), but that eternal life is subject to the sleep of death and will need to be resurrected. As John puts it, "the hour is coming in which all who are in the graves will hear His voice and come forth—those who have done good, to the resurrection of life, and those who have done evil, to the resurrection of condemnation" (John 5:28, 29, NKJV). What we find in John on the resurrection of the just is the same picture we find of that event in 1 Thessalonians 4:14-17. Those who have died in Jesus will be sleeping in their tombs until the Second Advent, at which time He will awake them (John 5:28; 1 Thess. 4:13-17), confer immortality upon

---

An Interpretive Key

In order more completely to understand Philippians 1:23, we should note that the Bible writers at times refer to two events together that may be separated by a long period of time. Compare, for example, Luke 4:17-19 with Isaiah 61:1, 2. Jesus only quoted part of Isaiah as being fulfilled in His day because the remainder would not happen until the Second Coming. See also John 5:28, 29 which gives no indication that the two resurrections the disciple mentions in one sentence are separated by 1,000 years, as he explains in Revelation 20:4-6.

---

them (1 Cor. 15:51-53), and take them home with Him (1 Thess. 4:14).

"Well, if that is true," we need to ask, "what about Paul's hinting that to die was to be with Christ (Phil. 1:23)?" There is no doubt about what Paul said. What we need to ask is what he meant. The first thing to recognize in Philippians 1:23 is that Paul verbalizes his desire to leave this present troubled existence and be with Christ, without reference to any lapse of time that may occur between the two events. But that verse does not teach that Paul expected to go to heaven at death. In other places he was very clear that he would not receive his reward until the Second Coming, when all God's people would get their rewards along with him at the same time (2 Tim. 4:8; cf. Heb. 11:39, 40).

In Philippians 1:23 the apostle states that the next thing he would know after departing (death) would be Christ coming in the clouds of heaven to raise the dead. At that time all God's saints together would "meet the Lord in the air" (1 Thess. 4:15-17). Until then all would sleep in their graves (verse 14), awaiting the awakening call of God (verse 16; John 5:28). In the meantime, they would remain in that deep, unconscious sleep, which is the Bible's way of describing death.

The Old Testament somewhat fills out the sleep metaphor for death. The psalmist proclaims that "the dead do not praise the Lord" (Ps. 115:17, NASB) and that when a person dies "his spirit departs, he returns to the earth; in that very day his thoughts perish" (Ps. 146:4, NASB). The Bible pictures death as a deep sleep in which the dead are unaware of what is transpiring, a sleep from which they will not awake until the resurrection.

Martin Luther, the fountainhead of the Reformation, held that understanding of death. "For," he wrote, "just as a man who falls asleep and sleeps soundly until morning does not know what has happened to him when he wakes up, so we shall suddenly rise on the Last Day; and we shall know neither what death has been like or how we have come through it." Again, he penned, "We are to sleep until he comes and knocks on the grave and says, 'Dr. Martin, get up.' Then I will arise in a moment and will be eternally happy with him" (Luther in Althaus, pp. 414, 415). Luther

> According to Martin Luther "it would take a foolish soul to desire its body when it was already in heaven" (Luther, in Althaus, p. 417).

scholar Paul Althaus indicates that "later Lutheran Church theology did not follow Luther on this point. Rather, it once again adopted the medieval tradition and continued it" (*ibid.*, 417).

The Bible picture of death as sleep until the resurrection exposes the tension between the nonbiblical doctrine of the immortality of the soul and the biblical teaching of the resurrection. It is no accident that leading twentieth-century Protestant theologian Oscar Cullman titled his Harvard lecture on the topic "Immortality of the Soul or Resurrection of the Dead." "The immortality of the soul," he argued, is "one of the greatest misunderstandings of Christianity. . . . The concept of death and resurrection is anchored in the Christ-event" and "is incompatible with the Greek belief in immortality." That Greek understanding, Cullmann demonstrates, is deeply rooted in Plato's *Phaedo* and other Greek thinkers (Cullmann, p. 9). Werner Jaeger in his Harvard lecture on the topic also highlights the fact that "the Immortality of Man was one of the fundamental creeds of the philosophical religion of Platonism that was in part adopted by the Christian church" (Jaeger, p. 97). And under the influence of Greek philosophy the Bible picture of the sleep of the dead and their resurrection at the end of time became confused in the minds of many.

But the clear teaching of 1 Thessalonians 4:13-18 is that the good news of Christianity is not merely that Jesus died and rose for His followers, but that He will come again so that they also can rise from the dead, meet Him in the air, and be taken to His heavenly kingdom. Thus Christians have hope for the future, joy in the present, and comfort across the ages, in spite of the problem of death.

17. Instruction on Second Advent Hope

1 Thessalonians 4:15-18

[15]*For this we say to you by the word of the Lord, that we who are living, who remain until the coming of the Lord, will most certainly not precede those who have fallen asleep.* [16]*Because the Lord Himself will descend from heaven with a shout, with the voice of an archangel, and with a trumpet of God, and the dead in Christ shall rise first.* [17]*Then we who are living, who remain, will be caught up together with them in the clouds to meet*

with the Lord in the air, and so will we always be with the Lord.
¹⁸Therefore comfort one another with these words.

With verses 15-17 we come to one of the most insightful pictures of the Second Advent recorded in the New Testament. But if we are to understand this snapshot of glory we need to remember that Paul's purpose is pastoral. He has not written to whet our speculative appetites for the fine points of eschatology or to provide us with a full and detailed list of events that will take place at the return of Christ. Rather, he is seeking to comfort a group of new believers who were deeply concerned about those of their number who had died and who were asking, "What will happen to them? Will they lose out on the great events to take place at the Second Coming?"

We have seen in verses 13 and 14 that Paul did not want them to be ignorant on the topic, and that just as Jesus rose from the grave so would His followers. Now in verses 15-17 the apostle wants to state plainly what he had only hinted at in verse 13.

He begins by alerting them to the fact that what he has to say is not his own thoughts on the topic, but is straight from Jesus Himself—it is "the word of the Lord" (verse 15). That is, he had a saying of Jesus on the topic as his authority. But here we have a problem, because we find no such saying in the New Testament. The closest we have is Matthew 24:31: "He will send out his angels with a loud trumpet call, and they will gather his elect from the four winds, from one end of heaven to the other" (RSV).

While that statement is similar, 1 Thessalonians 4:15-17 definitely contains important details that go beyond Matthew 24:31. Where did they come from? Here we need to remember that 1 Thessalonians is probably the earliest written Christian document that we possess. None of the Gospels had yet been put into writing. Rather, the apostles and their converts had committed the many details of Christ's life and His sayings to memory and were transmitting them orally. That would be the practice of the church until the four Gospels as we know them were written out by Matthew, Mark, Luke, and John between the 60s and 90s of the first Christian century. Not all of the genuine sayings of Jesus found their way into the Bible. John 21:25 is quite specific on that topic. What we have in 1 Thessalonians 4:15-17 is Paul citing the direct word of the Lord from that oral data bank. He does the same in 1 Corinthians 7:10, 25; 9:14; 11:23-25, and Acts 20:35. That was the only New Testament they had at that early period. Of course, the Gospels would eventually be written, and they, along with Paul's letters to the Thessalonians, would be collected into what today we call the New Testament.

The saying of the Lord that Paul reports in 1 Thessalonians 4:15-17 must have been extremely comforting to the distressed believers. For one thing, in verse 15 he lets them know that those who had died and were sleeping would have absolutely no disadvantage at the Second Advent. To the contrary, they would have the honor of firstness. The apostle notes that the living "will most certainly not precede those who have fallen asleep." He goes out of his way to emphasize his point by using an emphatic negative. Thus I have translated it as "most certainly not" rather than merely "not." Paul wants them to have complete assurance on the point that is troubling them. They were not to worry about those who died. God would not forget them.

The Order of Events in 1 Thessalonians 4:15-17

1. Jesus returns in the clouds of heaven.
2. The dead who are "in Christ" are resurrected.
3. Living Christians are caught up to meet both Christ and the resurrected believers in the air.

With verse 16 we can feel the excitement building up in Paul as he describes the coming itself. Not only will the Lord return from heaven as He had promised His earliest disciples (Acts 1:11), but He will do so with glory and fanfare. Far from being a secret event, it will be heard and seen across the face of the earth. In verse 15 Paul had spoken of the Lord's "coming" using the Greek word *parousia*, the term used when a king or other dignitary visited a city. That was quite appropriate, because in this case the honored person is no less than "the Lord Himself" (verse 16).

The royal *parousia* will be heralded in three ways. First, by a shout or command. Here we have a word used as an exclamation by a ship's master to his rowers, by a charioteer to his horses, and as a military battle cry. "In most places it denotes a loud, authoritative cry, often one uttered in the thick of great excitement" (Rogers, p. 479).

Second, the shout either is or accompanies "the voice of an

archangel." The Greek does not read "the archangel" because it has no article. Thus it mentions no specific archangel. However, the only other place "archangel" appears in the New Testament is in Jude 9, which speaks of "Michael the archangel," for which we have good evidence that it is referring to Christ (see Knight, *Letters*, pp. 255, 256). If that is the case here, we could surmise that the voice of the archangel is Christ calling forth the saints from their graves. While that picture is attractive, it is not spelled out in 1 Thessalonians 4:16. All the text mentions is "an archangel."

Third, beyond the shout and the voice of an archangel, verse 16 tells us that the *parousia* will also be announced by "a trumpet of God." To catch the significance of that phrase, we need to remember that in that era the trumpet was not primarily a musical instrument. To the contrary, it found its main role in announcing military exercises, religious events, and so on. In the Roman army nothing happened without the sounding of the trumpet. And in the Old Testament trumpets were often used in connection with times of festivity and triumph. Paul connects that instrument to the Second Advent in 1 Corinthians 15:52 in which he writes that "the trumpet will sound, and the dead will be raised imperishable, and we shall be changed" (RSV). The trumpet "fits in as part of the pageantry, stressing the majesty of the Lord and the greatness of the day" (Morris, *First and Second*, 1991, p. 144).

John Stott suggests that in verse 16 "we are probably not meant to imagine three distinct voices (the *command*, the *voice* and the *trumpet*) but rather to understand the variety and repetition as indicating the overwhelming, irresistible nature of the summons" (Stott, p. 102). Whatever the exact situation, one thing is clear. The second coming of Christ will be anything but secret.

The coming itself will not merely be something that takes place in the heavens. It will have earthly consequences. Jesus had forecasted while

A Rapture That Is Anything But Secret

It will be accompanied by:
1. A massive shout
2. The voice of an archangel
3. A trumpet announcement
Beyond that
4. His coming will be as visible as lightning that illuminates the sky from east to west (Matt. 24:27).
5. Every eye will see His coming (Rev. 1:7).

on earth that "the hour is coming in which all who are in the graves will hear His voice and come forth—those who have done good to the resurrection of life, and those who have done evil, to the resurrection of condemnation" (John 5:28, 29, NKJV). First Thessalonians 4:16 speaks to the first of those resurrections when it indicates that the dead "*in Christ*" would be called to life at the Second Coming. (The second resurrection will not take place until the end of the millennium—see Rev. 20:5, 7.)

The Thessalonians had been worried about whether their sleeping (dead) loved ones would miss out on something special at the Lord's return. Now they have their answer. They will have priority. First comes their resurrection. Then, Paul adds in verse 17, "we who are living . . . will be caught up together with them in the clouds to meet with the Lord in the air." Nobody is left out! The dead are raised to life and the living are caught up and they are united, nevermore to part. Comforting words to the Thessalonians and to us.

The word translated as "caught up" is of interest. It means "to seize," to "snatch away," and to "transport hastily" (Mounce, p. 1097). It has worked its way into English through the Latin *rapio* as "rapture." So when we hear someone speaking of the end-time rapture, we know that they have in mind God's people being caught up to meet Jesus at the end of time. But we also need to remember that there is absolutely nothing secret about the rapture. Nor are the saints raptured at a time different from the Second Advent or the resurrection of those dead who have been faithful to God through the ages. Paul is crystal clear on those points. It is important to let the Bible speak for itself rather than to read our theological ideas into it.

The apostle closes off his great passage on the Second Advent with the command to comfort one another on the basis of the truth that he has just presented. And comforting words they are. Christians have absolutely nothing to fear in death. Jesus conquered the grave, and He offers His victory to each of His followers.

As we read 1 Thessalonians 4:13-18, we need to remember the passage's practical nature in Paul's day and ours. "This," Gene Green insightfully writes, "is not the stuff of speculative prophecy or bestsellers on the end times. The text is located at the funeral home, the memorial service, and the graveside. It is placed in the hands of each believer to comfort others in their time of greatest sorrow. The decidedly bizarre pictures of airplanes dropping out of the sky and cars careening out of control as the rapture happens detract from the hope that this passage is designed to teach. The picture presented here is of the royal coming of Jesus Christ. The church, as the official delegation, goes out to meet him, with the dead heading up the procession as those most honored. One coming is envisioned, which will unite the coming King with his subjects. What a glorious hope!" (Green, p. 229). AMEN!

18. Instruction on the Timing of the Day of the Lord

1 Thessalonians 5:1-3

¹Now concerning the times and the dates, brothers, you have no need for anything to be written to you. ²For you yourselves know well that the day of the Lord will come like a thief in the night. ³While they are saying, "Peace and safety," then sudden destruction will come upon them like birth pains to a woman having a child, and they will certainly not escape.

Two problems have particularly troubled people through the ages. The first is What happens at death? or What is the meaning of death? The second has to do with the end of the world and being ready for that event. Paul dealt with the first issue in 1 Thessalonians 4:13-18. He will now in chapter 5 face the second. Thus while there is a relationship between 1 Thessalonians 4:13-18 and 5:1-11, it would be wrong to see chapter 5 as a mere continuation of the earlier material. The fact that he is taking up a new issue Paul signals by his "now concerning . . . brothers," a formula he had earlier used in 1 Thessalonians 4:9 and 13 to begin the treatment of a new question that the Thessalonian believers had forwarded to him through Timothy.

First Thessalonians 5:1 introduces the new topic when Paul notes that "concerning the times and the dates" he has no need to write to them. We must explore two items in that verse. The first is the meaning of "the times and the dates," a phrase that verse 2 will connect with "the day of the Lord." Here we find a perennial question. When will the end come? When will Jesus return? The Thessalonians seemed to be obsessed with the issue, as 2 Thessalonians 2:1-3 indicates when Paul again addresses the topic.

The question was not new with the Thessalonians. It had stimulated Jesus' sermon on the Second Advent in Matthew 24, 25 when the disciples asked, "Tell us, . . . what will be the sign of your coming and of the close of the age" (Matt. 24:3, RSV). In terms of "the times and the dates," Jesus was not as helpful as the disciples wished Him to be. "Of that day and hour," Jesus told them, "no one knows . . . but the Father only" (verse 36, RSV). At the time of His ascension Jesus repeated that answer in response to a similar question. "He said to them, 'It is not for you to know times or seasons ["the times and the dates" of 1 Thessalonians 5:1] which the Father has fixed by his own authority'" (Acts 1:7. RSV). Jesus sought to lead His followers away from an unhealthy fixation on dates and toward being ready for the event when it finally takes place (see Matt. 24:45-25:46). Paul will do the same in 1 Thessalonians 5:1-11.

The second thing we need to observe about verse 1 is that the apostle claims that he had no need to write them on the topic, presumably because they had already been thoroughly instructed on it. That was true, but Paul did comment on the topic. Why? Probably because their intellectual selves were being confused by their emotional selves. As noted in our treatment of chapter 4, they had been deeply disturbed that some of their fellow believers had died before the Second Coming. Their anguish led them to wonder about their own futures and whether they would be ready for the event. Paul in his pastoral role addresses their concerns in chapter 5.

In verse 2 the apostle reinforces in a positive manner what he had told them in a negative one in verse 1. Here he states that they know the truth about "the day of the Lord" rather than that they needed no instruction on the topic. Their knowledge on the subject was firm, but he will still give them a refresher course beginning in verse 3.

Meanwhile the readers' attention is drawn to the phrase "day of the Lord" in verse 2. Here is a term pregnant with meaning in both the Old and New Testaments. On the one hand, the Old Testament pictures the "day of the Lord" as a time of judgment. Thus the prophet Amos writes in the eighth century B.C.: "Woe to you who desire the day of the Lord! Why would you have the day of the Lord? It is darkness, and not light; as if a man fled from a lion, and a bear met him. . . . Is not the day of the Lord darkness, and not light, and gloom with no brightness in it?" (Amos 5:18-20, RSV). And Isaiah tells his readers to "wail, for the day of the Lord is near; as destruction from the Almighty it will come!" (Isa. 13:6, RSV). Joel refers to it as "the great and terrible day of the Lord" (Joel 2:31, RSV; see also Eze. 13:5; 30:3; Joel 1:15-2:1, 11; 3:14; Zeph. 1:7, 14; Zech. 14:1; Mal. 4:5).

But the Old Testament day of the Lord wasn't focused only on judgment. It was also one of salvation. As a result, Joel moves on from his description of "the great and terrible day of the Lord" to proclaim that on that day "all who call upon the name of the Lord shall be delivered" (Joel 2:32, RSV). We see that salvation motif for the day of the Lord also graphically portrayed in Zechariah 14:1-21 and Obadiah 15-21.

> "At the center of redemption past is Christ on the cross; at the center of redemption future is Christ returning in glory" (Ladd, p. 6).

That same picture of the day of the Lord appears in the New Testament, in which it still has the two-edged significance as being both a day of salvation for God's people and a day of final reckoning for the wicked. But the New Testament often abbreviates the Old Testament "day of the Lord" to "day." Thus 2 Peter 2:9 can refer to it as "the day of judgment," Romans 2:5 as the day of God's wrath, Ephesians 4:30 as "the day of redemption," 2 Thessalonians 1:10 as "that day," John 6:39, 40 as "the last day," and Jude 6 as "the great day." That "day," of course, is the Second Advent, when "the Son of man is to come with his angels in the glory of his Father, and then he will repay every man for what he has done" (Matt. 16:27, RSV). It will be good news for those "in Christ" (1 Thess. 4:16), but bad for those found rejecting God and His will. For believers in Christ, it will signify redemption completed.

The significance of the day of the Lord was apparently clear enough to the Thessalonian converts. What bothered them was its timing. Paul's advice echoes that of Jesus who told people to watch (Matt. 24:42) and be ready (verse 44) because no one knows when it will come (verse 36), but that it would take place at a time they did not expect it (verse 44).

The apostle picks up on the unexpected time theme in 1 Thessalonians 5:2 and 3, using two illustrations. The first is that of the thief, one employed by Jesus in Matthew 24:43 and in several other places in the New Testament (see, e.g., 2 Peter 3:10; Rev. 3:3; 16:15). Thieves, of course, do not make advance announcements about the time of their arrival. The same will be true of Jesus' return. The second illustration is that of a woman about to give birth. She knows it will take place but doesn't know when, until she feels the first labor pains.

Both illustrations share the same suddenness of their arrival. But they are different in that one is unexpected while the other is anticipated but unavoidable. Thus in the first illustration there will be no warning, and in the second no way of escape.

The result is that "sudden destruction" will come at the very time some are announcing "Peace and safety," that there is no reason for concern. Second Peter 3:3, 4 highlights that same relaxed attitude when it predicts the presence of "scoffers . . . in the last days" who follow their own passions and ask, "Where is the promise of his coming? For ever since the fathers fell asleep, all things have continued as they were from the beginning of creation" (RSV).

There have always been those who have cried "Peace and safety" and who have turned the attention of men and women away from "the day of the Lord" and back to the pleasures and ways of earthly life. False prophets prophesying peace had preceded Judah's judgment in Jeremiah 6:14 and other places. And in the Roman world of the Thessalonians "*pax et securitas* ('peace and safety') was a popular slogan of the imperial" government, even being stamped on their coins. "Rome held out to all those who submitted to its rule the promise of peace and safety, virtually an offer of 'salvation' from unrest and danger" (Weima, p. 424).

But Paul had a different message: don't trust the powers of this world with all of their promises. "Sudden destruction" will overwhelm them and all they stand for in "the day of the Lord" (1 Thess. 5:3). It will strike unexpectedly like a thief and suddenly like labor pains, but it will come. And from that thought the apostle leads his readers into the necessity of staying awake and being prepared for the event in verses 4 to 11. There is no reason, his logic runs, why the Second Advent should catch a Christian off guard.

19. Instruction on How to Live Until the Day of the Lord

1 Thessalonians 5:4-11

⁴But you, brothers, are not in darkness, that the day should overtake you as a thief. ⁵For you are all sons of light and sons of day. We are not of night or of darkness. ⁶So then let us not sleep as others do, but let us keep awake and be sober. ⁷For those who sleep sleep by night, and those who get drunk are drunk at night. ⁸But since we are of the day, let us be sober, having clothed ourselves with the breastplate of faith and love and as a helmet the hope of salvation. ⁹Because God has not appointed us to wrath, but to obtaining salvation through our Lord Jesus Christ, ¹⁰the one who died for us, so that whether we are awake or are sleeping, we will live together with Him. ¹¹Therefore comfort one another and build up each other, just as you are doing.

The theme of 1 Thessalonians 5:4-11 is how Christians should live as they await "the day of the Lord" (verse 2). The previous verses had indicated that it would arrive like a thief in the night. People might be crying "Peace and safety," but inescapable "sudden destruction" would come upon them when they least expected it (verses 2, 3).

Verse 4 reverts to the thief motif as the letter moves from generalities about the day of the Lord to specifics in regard to the Thessalonian believers as they looked forward to that event. We can outline the flow of verses 4-11 as follows.

1. Two spiritual locations—light and darkness (verses 4, 5).
2. Two ways of life based upon the two spiritual locations (verses 6-8).
3. Two destinies related to both the two spiritual locations, the two ways of life, and the grace of God through Christ (verses 9, 10).

The main distinction in verses 4 and 5 is between those living in darkness and those living in the light. The day of the Lord will catch the first group by surprise because they are sleeping, while the second group, being awake, will be prepared for that event (verse 6).

In order to understand the passage we must first catch the significance of darkness and light in the Bible. All the way through Scripture we find a "conflict between light and darkness" (Ryken, pp. 509, 191), with light representing the forces of good, and darkness those of evil. Thus darkness symbolizes the dominion of sin that rules the lives of the unconverted (John 3:19; Eph. 5:11) whose minds have been darkened (Rom. 1:21). Within that framework, the New Testament pictures salvation as moving from darkness to light (Eph. 5:8; 1 Peter 2:9). The Christian, therefore, is one who has exited the realm of darkness and entered that of light.

That light, Paul tells his readers in verses 4 and 5, has two effects on believers. First, pointing back to verses 2 and 3, it enlightens their minds so that they will not be surprised by the coming of the day of the Lord. Second, pointing forward to verses 6-8, the light informs their conduct as they prepare for that event.

The "so then" of verse 6 shifts the scene from a discussion of Christians being children of light rather than darkness and toward the impact that light will have on their lives. And in doing so Paul shifts from using the second person plural to the first person plural. He begins the transition in verse 5, in which he writes "*you* are all sons of light. . . . *We* are not of the night." He will continue to use the first person plural up through the end of verse 10, thus gently drawing "the Thessalonians into the common Christian life, reminding them of who *we* are and what *we* do" (Green, p. 237).

The contrast in verses 6-8 is between those who sleep and are drunk with those who live soberly and live a life of awareness of spiritual things. Taken together, we need not interpret sleeping and drunkenness in their most literal meaning, but rather in the sense of partaking in "the prevailing habits of non-Christian life" (Ellicott, p. 71). People with those characteristics, Paul asserts in verse 7, belong to the realm of darkness.

The "but since we are of the day" at the beginning of verse 8 refocuses our attention from the children of darkness and toward those who exist in the light and lead "sober" lives. The point emphasized here is the intimate relationship between the new existence of Christians and their new moral life. Here we encounter a theme that runs all the way through Paul's writings and even throughout the entire New Testament—becoming a Christian leads to a new way of life. In other words, "getting saved" is not something that merely happens in people's inner being but is an experience that finds expression in how they live their lives. Repeatedly we find that pattern reflected in Paul's letters. Thus Romans, Galatians, Ephesians, and other epistles consistently move from theological concerns related to salvation to ethical issues in daily living. Herman Ridderbos identifies that move as the shift from the "indicative" to the "imperative," from declarations about the process of salvation to commands as to how salvation will affect a Christian's life (Ridderbos, 253-258). As a result, Paul constantly teaches that the gift of grace includes the call to obedience.

Those living the night life of sleepiness (being unaware) and drunkenness (being totally inebriated and consumed by the affairs of this life) will be caught unaware by the coming of the Lord. They will be surprised, as with a thief in the night (verse 2). But, we read in verse 8, that will not be the case of those who are "sober." Such individuals, aware of the true significance of what is taking place around them, are preparing for the eschaton by living in the light of God's word.

In the middle of verse 8 Paul shifts the metaphor away from light and darkness and their accompanying awakeness and sleepiness and toward military imagery. But in his mind he did not see the two as being radically different. Rather, the apostle probably viewed the light versus darkness metaphor as naturally flowing into conflict of a military nature. After all,

> ## Balanced Christianity
>
> "Genuine Christian faith has an 'eschatological edge' that balances vivid hope about the future with stellar piety in the present" (Green, p. 246).

"the power of darkness in the NT is so vivid that it is more than a symbol, becoming nothing less than a spiritual reality. Jesus himself spoke of 'the power of darkness' (Lk. 22:53), and Paul spoke of how Christians do not battle against physical enemies but against 'the cosmic powers of this present darkness, against the spiritual forces of evil in the heavenly places' (Eph. 6:12, NRSV)" (Ryken, p. 192).

It was in the context of that spiritual battle in Ephesians 6 that the apostle set forth his memorable description of the Christian being clothed in "the whole armor of God" (Eph. 6:13-17). First Thessalonians 5:8 presents an abbreviated exposition of that armor. The apostle has believers clothed "with the breastplate of faith and love and as a helmet the hope of salvation." In relation to the overall message of 1 Thessalonians, it is believers' faith in God, love toward Him and other people, and their hope in the Second Advent that prepares them for that event. We should note that 1 Thessalonians deliberately connects hope with a Christian's belief in the return of Jesus and the resurrection of the saints. Thus Paul contrasts hope with those who have "no hope" (1 Thess. 4:13). Having remained awake, having lived sober and responsible lives, and having put on the armor of salvation, the Thessalonian believers will be ready for "the day of the Lord." And we in the twenty-first century will be also if we heed the apostle's counsel.

The "because" in verse 9 indicates the next stage in Paul's presentation. Up to this point in verses 4-8 he has outlined the two spiritual realms in which people exist and how each leads to different ways of life. In verse 9 he turns to the two destinies that await the two spiritual and life orientations that he has spelled out in the previous verses: wrath or "salvation through our Lord Jesus Christ."

Verses 9 and 10 emphasize the salvation aspect of the dichotomy rather than the fate of the wicked (highlighted in 1 Thessalonians 2:16 and especially 2 Thessalonians 1:7-9 and 2:8-10). Paul in verse 9 does not mean that God predestined some people to wrath and others to salvation. To the contrary, it is God's will that all come to salvation, but they have to make a Spirit-inspired choice to accept His offer. John's Gospel spells that out when it says that "God so loved the world that he gave his only Son, that *whoever believes* in him should not perish but have eternal life" (John 3:16, RSV). It is God's part to make the provision in Christ's dying "once for all" (Heb. 10:10, 14). And it is our part to accept God's gift in Christ through His gift of faith (Rom. 3:23-25). The Bible picture is one of God appointing all people for salvation, a gift that some accept and others reject (John 3:36). The latter group are "appointed" or "destined" (RSV) for wrath, while those who accept have salvation as their destination.

First Thessalonians 5:10 is one of the few verses in the Thessalonian correspondence that mentions the cross of Christ (see also 2:15; 4:14), and the only place that explains the purpose of His death. That purpose was that we might find eternal life in Him whether we have died and need to be resurrected (1 Thess. 4:16) or will meet Him in the air after being raptured at the time of His coming (4:17). All believers whether they are "asleep" (dead) at that time or "awake" (alive) will participate in that event. Thus the apostle has returned to his argument of 1 Thessalonians 4:13-18, in which he dealt with the fear of the Thessalonian believers that those among their number who had died would lose out at the great day of the Lord's appearing. And as in the discussion of the topic in chapter 4, Paul concludes his present treatment in 5:11 with the same command: "Comfort one another and build up each other" in the blessed certainty of the return of Jesus, the resurrection of the Christian dead, and their reunion with the living when they meet Jesus in the air (1 Thess. 4:14-17).

And what does Paul's counsel in 1 Thessalonians 5:4-11 mean for those who live in the twenty-first century? The same as it did for those in the first. Don't get so concerned with the affairs of this world of darkness that you lose sight of the eternal, and don't forget the fact that all of those things that we value so much will pass away. In short, that we do not let our desire for well-being in the present world lead us to neglect preparation for that great event of the future, which will be the ultimate victory and experience.

20. Instruction Regarding Life in the Christian Community

1 Thessalonians 5:12-18

[12]*Now we request of you, brothers, to appreciate those who labor among you and exercise leadership over you in the Lord and admonish you,* [13]*and to esteem them very highly in love because of their work. Be at peace among yourselves.* [14]*And we encourage you, brothers, admonish the disorderly, encourage the fainthearted, help the weak, be patient with all.* [15]*See that no one repays anyone evil for evil, but always eagerly seek the good for one another and for everyone.* [16]*Rejoice always,* [17]*pray unceasingly,* [18]*give thanks in everything. For this is God's will for you in Christ Jesus.*

Thus far in the instructional part of 1 Thessalonians, which began in 4:1, Paul has provided two levels of material. First, moral instruction largely related to sexual purity based on Timothy's report to Paul about the problems in the Thessalonian church (4:1-8). Second, instruction on three questions that the Thessalonians themselves wanted answered (4:9-12; 13-18; 5:1-11). Now in 1 Thessalonians 5:12-22 the apostle turns to a third instructional category of a more general nature but one centering on how to behave in the Christian community.

What is difficult to determine in verses 12 through 22 is whether the material it contains is instruction meant for all congregations or whether Paul specifically developed it for the needs of the Thessalonian community. In favor of the first alternative, Ernest Best points out that most of the counsel "is very general and is derived probably from traditional material" taught to every congregation about Christian behavior. To support that perspective, he notes that 1 Thessalonians 5:12-22 mostly contains the same material as Romans 12:9-21 (Best, p. 223).

Arguing the second alternative on the nature of the advice in verses 12-22, I. Howard Marshall observes that while "a common basis in tradition exists," given the similarities to Romans 12, "it is arguable that he shaped the teaching to suit the needs of each individual community. . . . It would indeed be improbable that Paul should write in general terms to a church of which he had particular knowledge and at the end of a letter which has throughout been directly and closely applied to their specific situation" (Marshall, p. 146).

What we probably have in 1 Thessalonians 5:12-22 is a standard instructional curriculum containing matters suitable for all congregations, but also containing a list of items framed to meet the specific needs of the Thessalonian congregation. Thus just because Paul tells them to "rejoice always" and to "pray unceasingly" (verses 16, 17), that does not mean that the Thessalonians were a sad-faced, prayerless congregation. Rather, those were general admonitions that Paul repeatedly gave to the congregations he founded. On the other hand, the counsel related to respecting the congregation's leadership (verses 12, 13) and the issue of "the disorderly" (verse 14, "idlers," RSV) appears to be much more appropriate to the Thessalonian church and does not appear in parallel passages.

The instruction in verses 12-22 divides into four categories:

1. Instruction on respecting church leadership (verses 12, 13).
2. Instruction on living together as a congregation (verses 14, 15).
3. Instruction on general spiritual life (verses 16-18).
4. Instruction related to evaluating those claiming the prophetic gift (verses 19-22).

In regard to leadership, 1 Thessalonians 5:12, 13 requests the believers to appreciate, love, and respect the leaders of their congregation because of their responsibilities. That counsel echoes that in Hebrews 13:17, which commands Christians to "obey your leaders and submit to them; for they are keeping watch over your souls, as men who will have to give an account" (RSV). The leadership advice also reflects in a general way the counsel in the letters to Timothy and Titus.

The very presence of counsel on honoring leadership implies that there existed a problem in that area in the Thessalonian church. It is probable that some of the members were resisting the leaders of the local congregation in the realm of sexual purity (4:1-8). That continuing problem is one reason the apostle had to deal firmly with the topic. Another area in which some of the congregation disregarded the instruction of the local leadership involved their not working or "disorderly" conduct (1 Thess. 5:14; 4:11; 2 Thess. 3:11).

The leaders themselves were undoubtedly local elders. "The first groups of Christians," Leon Morris points out, "seem to have been organized on the model of the synagogue . . . , and thus would have had a group of elders exercising oversight" (Morris, *First and Second*, 1991, p. 164). In fact, James 2:2 calls a Christian "church" (TLB), "assembly" (NASB), or "place of worship" (NEB) a synagogue (*synagōgē*). It appears that the earliest Christians built upon the synagogue model in forming local congregations. Thus we find Paul and his fellow missionaries had "appointed elders . . . in every church" (Acts 14:23, RSV). It was probably the authority of those local elders that Paul speaks about in 1 Thessalonians 5:12, 13.

Here is counsel greatly needed for church members in the twenty-first century. We live in an era in which personal correction "has almost become anathema in the church" (Green, p. 250). But that was never Paul's ideal. To the contrary, one of the functions of Christian leaders is to "admonish" or instruct the congregation as they need correction in the realms of doctrine and morals. Such faithful leaders are to be appreciated and "highly" esteemed (verse 13).

Moving on from the theme of loyalty to church leadership (verses 12, 13), Paul next turns to the mutual care of various individuals within the congregation to each other. Here he is not speaking of the functions of leadership, but of the role of every member in creating a healthy Christian community.

> The responsibility of every Christian is to:
> 1. "*admonish* the disorderly,"
> 2. "*encourage* the fainthearted,"
> 3. "*help* the weak,"
> 4. "*be patient* with all," and
> 5. "always eagerly *seek the good* for one another and for everyone" (1 Thess. 5:14, 15).

With the words "admonish," "encourage," "help," "be patient," and "seek the good" we find a description of the ministry of every church member to every other member, to the church as a collection of individuals, and even to the larger community outside of the church. Spectator Christianity is not a part of the apostolic view of the church. We don't belong to a church merely to hear once a week a preacher preach much like an actor acts or an entertainer entertains, but to be productive, working members in the family of God. Each of us has a ministry to enrich and heal and maintain the good health of the congregation. It is high time that some of us stopped complaining about the problems in the church as if it were "them" who were responsible. Open your eyes! Read your Bible! Paul tells us that each of us has a serious function in the overall health of the body of the church.

While encouraging the fainthearted in a church undergoing persecution certainly speaks to the situation in Thessalonica, probably the most specific counsel Paul makes to that particular congregation is that of admonishing the disorderly. The Greek word I translated "disorderly" is rendered as "idlers" in many Bibles (e.g. RSV). George Milligan notes that the Greek word is "primarily a military term applied to the soldier who does not remain in the ranks, and thence used more generally of whatever is out of order. In the present passage the special reference would seem to be to the idleness and neglect of duty which characterized certain members of the Thessalonian Church in view of the shortly-expected Parousia"

(Milligan, p. 73). Another aspect of that disorderliness would be those out of line in the area of sexual immorality (1 Thess. 4:1-8). Because of the Greek word's broader meaning related to anything out of order, I translated it as "disorderly," a term that includes the problem of "idlers" (RSV), but is not restricted to them. On the other hand, it is easy to see why some have rendered the term as "idlers," since members of the congregation who were "out of order" in the realm of work were an ongoing problem among the Thessalonian believers (see 1 Thess. 4:11; 2 Thess. 3:11). But disorderliness includes more than idleness. It encompasses all the ways in which Christians are out of harmony with their divine Commander.

Another way in which some of the Thessalonian Christians may have been "disorderly" in the face of the admonitions of their leaders could have been in the area of retribution. There may have been some with a vengeful spirit determined to get even with other church members. While that cannot be proven, it is a general problem in most churches, and its antidote of being a blessing to everyone is a perennial need of every person and every congregation (verse 15).

Paul closes his counsel of general advice in verses 16-18 with a rapid-fire trinity of admonitions for a healthy spiritual life in all ages and all places for all Christians. First, he exhorts, "rejoice always." Good counsel, especially in the light of the Second Advent and resurrection featured in chapters 4 and 5. Christians have more to rejoice about than anyone else in the world. We should do it more. Too often we grumble instead of rejoicing. If we followed Paul's counsel and rejoiced always it would transform our lives and our influence.

Second, "pray unceasingly." Prayer is not something for church or morning and evening worship. To the contrary, Paul exhorts, we need to practice it in all of life's activities. We can be in an attitude of prayer and of communication with God as we drive down the road, talk to friends, or any other activity. The source of boundless comfort and wisdom is with us at all times if we desire it.

Third, "give thanks in everything," even those problems and pains that we see as disasters but which God uses for our growth in character and spiritual things (Rom. 5:3-5; Luke 6:23). We serve a God who can even make good come out of the problems in our lives (Rom. 8:28). He says to each of us, "My grace is sufficient for you, for my power is made perfect in weakness." And Paul reports of himself, "When I am weak, then I am strong" (2 Cor. 12:9, 10, RSV). Christians can truly be thankful for "everything"—for the good things in their lives for obvious reasons, but also for the not so good that God uses for good anyway.

With such a God in our lives we can truly "rejoice always, pray unceasingly, [and] give thanks in everything" (verses 16, 17). What a God! Amen!

21. Instruction Related to the Gift of Prophecy

1 Thessalonians 5:19-22

[19]Do not quench the Spirit; [20]do not despise prophetic activity. [21]But test all things; hold fast that which is good; [22]keep away from every form of evil.

Paul concludes his list of practical exhortations that began in 1 Thessalonians 5:12 with five staccato sayings all dealing with the prophetic gift. "Why such an outburst?" we are forced to ask. The only answer is that tensions over the topic must have disturbed the Thessalonian congregation. As a result, some in the congregation prohibited any prophetic activity. Thus here we find the opposite problem from that of the Corinthian church. In the latter Paul counseled those going to excess to slow down, but in Thessalonica it appears that some had clamped down so hard on the gifts that they were hindering the Holy Spirit's proper work. The apostle's inspired advice in 1 Thessalonians 5:19-21 is to move with care, and not to reject the gift outright. And with good reason, since "the prophet appears to have stood second only to the apostle if the Pauline order is to be taken seriously (1 Cor. 12:28; Eph. 4:11; 2:20)" (Hawthorne, p. 758).

Verse 19 finds the apostle confronting the problem head on. He commands them not to "quench the Spirit." Such places as Matthew 12:20, Ephesians 6:16, and Hebrews 11:34 employ "quench" for putting out a fire. And since the Holy Spirit is often associated with fire (Matt. 3:11; Acts 2:3), the word "quench" is especially appropriate. "Don't extinguish the work of the Holy Spirit," is the command. "He has a work to do until the end of time." Paul tells the Ephesians that the Spirit's gifts will be active in the church as long as its mission on earth lasts (Eph. 4:8-13). Some in the modern period, unfortunately, have failed to recognize that truth through a misreading of 1 Corinthians 13:8-12, which does indeed predict an end to the prophetic gift. But a reading of the passage makes it clear that the cessation takes place only "as an eschatological event" (Green, p. 262). Until that time we need to be wary of extinguishing the role of the Holy Spirit through the gifts that He supplies to the church.

Here we need to listen to Paul, even if we are a bit squeamish on the whole topic of spiritual gifts or the prophetic role being exercised in the church. Anglican scholar William Neil, who is personally cautious on the issue of the Spirit's gifts in the modern church, counsels that the apostle's words should "tend to make us hesitant in the life of the Church to-day before we condemn forms of religious expression with which we may not sympathize" (Neil, *St. Paul's Epistles*, p. 117).

While verse 19 does not identify the problematic gift in the Thessalonian context, verse 20 does: "do not despise prophetic activity." Here I need to point out that Thessalonica was not the only place in the ancient world where the gift of prophecy raised difficulties. The Old Testament indicates that false prophets were an ongoing problem. Jeremiah and other genuine prophets had to confront "prophets" whose counsel did not come from God and whose messages contradicted His Word to His people (see, e.g., 2 Chron. 18:5, 9, 20-22; Jer. 2:8; 5:31).

That phenomenon was not merely an Old Testament one. The *Didache*, which dates most likely to around A.D. 70-80, a time at which many of the New Testament books had not yet been written, highlights the problem of false prophets in the apostolic church. "Not everyone who speaks in the spirit is a prophet," it claims, "but only if he exhibits the Lord's ways." Interestingly enough, the *Didache* follows Paul's command to the Thessalonians to evaluate those who claim to have the prophetic gift. "If his teaching contributes to righteousness and knowledge of the Lord, welcome him as you would the Lord." But that test by itself is not enough. Prophets' lives must line up with their message. "If any prophet teaches the truth, yet does not practice what he teaches, he is a false prophet." Again, "by his conduct, therefore, will the false prophet and the [true] prophet be recognized." Especially problematic in the apostolic period were those traveling "prophets" who sought to sponge off the hospitality of the churches. As a result, the *Didache* warns, "if anyone should say in the spirit, 'Give me money,' or anything else, do not listen to him" (*Didache*, 11:1-11).

The particular form of prophetic abuse in the Thessalonian church most likely related to end-time events. Paul specifically raises that thought in 2 Thessalonians 2:2, which advises the church not to be "alarmed by some prophecy . . . saying that the day of the Lord has already come" (NIV). The specific problem alluded to in 2 Thessalonians, of course, most probably had developed between the writing of the two letters. But it is a "likely interpretation, given the conflict over prophetic utterances already attested to in 1 Thessalonians 5:19-20," that the problem with the prophetic gift in both Thessalonian letters had its origin in "eschatological prophecy" (Gillespie, pp. 47, 48). The fact that throughout the history of the church end-time excitement has often accompanied revivals of prophetic emphasis does seem to reinforce that idea.

Before leaving the topic of prophetic activity raised in 1 Thessalonians 5:20, we need to take a closer look at what the New Testament means by "prophecy." Leon Morris raises the issue when he points out that "it is often thought today that prophecy in the early church was more or less like preaching today." He claims that while the idea has some validity, "the essence of prophecy as the early church understood it appears to have been that the Spirit of the Lord spoke to and through people. Prophecy was one of the gifts of the Spirit (1 Cor. 12:10); a prophet speaks because 'a revelation' (1 Cor. 14:30) had been made to him" (Morris, *First and Second*, 1991, p. 177).

The problem faced by genuine prophetic activity is that it "lent itself to imitation" (Bruce, p. 125). Thus the need to be able to distinguish the claims of true prophets from the false. With that in mind, Paul tells his readers that they should not automatically reject the claims of a prophet (verse 20), but to test them (verse 21). Here we have a statement of caution following one affirmation: that is, don't automatically reject, but don't automatically accept. In short, in the face of a prophetic claim, jettison your emotional reaction, use common sense, and examine the claim "carefully" (1 Thess. 5:21, NASB). The Greek word (*dokimazō*), which I translated as "test" can also be rendered as "prove," "examine," or "scrutinize."

Greek writers often used it in connection with metals to discover if they are the real thing or counterfeits (Thayer, p. 155). Peter employs *dokimazō* that way when he speaks in relation to faith being like "gold which though perishable is tested by fire" (1 Peter 1:7, RSV).

Paul doesn't present any specific tests in 1 Thessalonians, but the New Testament suggests several, some of which, as we saw above, the authors of the *Didache* applied to contemporary prophets. According to G. K. Beale, those test include:

1. "The consistency of the prophecy with revealed Scripture (in Paul's time, the Old Testament [Acts 17:11]);
2. "the prophet's acknowledgment of Christ's full deity and humanity (1 Jn 4:1-6) as well as God's free forgiveness through Christ's death and resurrection (1 Cor 15:12-20; Gal 1:1-9);
3. "the godly character of the one claiming to be a prophet (Mt 7:15-23); and
4. "the result of the prophecy, which should always build up the church in every way (cf. 1 Cor 13-14)" (Beale, *1-2 Thessalonians*, pp. 174, 175).

> ## "Do Not Despise Prophetic Activity"
>
> "Abuses of ecstatic prophecy . . . must not be allowed to provoke any reaction which would depreciate and extinguish this vital gift or function of the faith. Paul, with characteristic sanity, holds the balance even. Such enthusiastic outbursts are neither to be despised as silly vapouring nor to be accepted blindly as infallible revelations" (Moffatt, p. 42).

When they have examined the prophetic claim and the results are in, Paul commands his readers to either "hold fast" or "keep away" from such prophetic activity. With one who claims to be a prophet, according to Paul, there is no middle ground. Their message is either to be wholeheartedly accepted or decisively rejected. Either their claim to be a prophet lines up with the biblical tests and is genuine or it fails (1 Thess. 5:21, 22).

The good news about 1 Thessalonians 5:19-22 is that Christians serve a God who still acts through the Holy Spirit to guide His church in the twenty-first century. He who led His people in Bible times is yet·with His people today and is still willing to bestow spiritual gifts upon His church as He sees fit in times of need. The prophecy of Joel 2:28-31 indicates that such guidance will especially be active as the day of the Lord approaches. Such a statement would have sounded familiar to the new believers in Thessalonica. But so would be the commands not to despise prophetic activity, but to thoroughly test all prophetic claimants, and to hold tightly to that which is genuine while rejecting the false. That counsel is just as important to the church today as it was to those first believers more than 2,000 years ago.

Part IV

Closing Matters

1 Thessalonians 5:23-28

22. Final Blessing and Sanctification in the Superlative

1 Thessalonians 5:23, 24

[23]Now may the God of peace Himself sanctify you entirely, and may your spirit and soul and body be preserved complete and blameless at the coming of our Lord Jesus Christ. [24]The one calling you is faithful, and He will accomplish it.

Paul begins and ends his letter in the same way—with a prayer. The opening prayer was one of thanksgiving for the Thessalonians' faithfulness and steadfastness (1 Thess. 1:2, 3). The closing prayer is in essence that God will continue His good work in them and bring it to completion (1 Thess. 5:23, 24).

In this prayer in the form of a wish, Paul addresses his petition to the "God of peace." Here we find a favorite expression of the apostle, especially in the final portions of his letters (see, e.g., Rom. 15:33; 2 Cor. 13:11; Phil. 4:9). The Christian concept of peace comes from the Hebrew *shalom*, a term much broader than the absence of conflict or war. Rather, *shalom* means complete well-being. In Romans 5:1 Paul notes that God brings peace into our lives because He justifies us and sets us free from the penalty of sin. But in its present context the concept of peace moves beyond the realm of justification. The *Jewish New Testament Commentary* suggests that in verse 23 "the essence of peace is . . . holiness, which means living a life centered on and guided by God" (Stern, p. 625). Another way of saying the same thing is that a Christian is walking through life in harmony with God and His will.

The role of God in a Christian's sanctification forms the very center of Paul's message in verses 23 and 24. Sanctification is a topic the apostle has already raised in 1 Thessalonians 3:13 and 4:3-8. In the first of those verses he prayed that God might establish the Thessalonians' "hearts blameless in holiness before our God and Father at the coming of our Lord Jesus." The first thing one notes about that passage when comparing it with 1 Thessalonians 5:23 is the similar wording and the fact that both passages emphasize holiness in relation to the Second Advent. The sanctification passage in chapter 4 highlights living in holiness in an immoral culture. The concluding verse suggests that God gives His followers the Holy Spirit to enable them to achieve spiritual victory (verse 8). That thought also underlies 1 Thessalonians 5:24, which asserts that victory will come through God as His people stay connected to Him.

> **God Expects Total Holiness**
>
> "Paul doesn't suggest that only a reasonable amount of holiness is required; it must be complete. Some Christians, emphasizing the boundless love of God and the doctrine of *justification by faith* apart from works, run the risk of underestimating the call of holiness, which Paul—who is after all the great exponent of God's love and of free justification—never did" (Wright, p. 134).

To emphasize his point about the need for holiness, Paul makes it twice in verse 23. First, he prays that God might sanctify them "entirely." As we noted earlier, the essential idea in sanctification is that of being set apart for God. But that is not merely an abstraction. It is a set apartness for holiness. As God is holy, so His followers are to be holy, which includes being different from or separated from the values and practices of what the Bible calls "the world." As a result, as James Frame points out, verse 23 is speaking about more than just "devotion to God." It also has to do with "conduct, ethical soundness" (Frame, p. 210).

The topic of the entire sanctification of the believer is so important to Paul that he repeats the idea in different words in the second half of verse 23: "May your spirit and soul and body be preserved complete and blameless at the coming of our Lord Jesus Christ." Here we find something in which people go off in strange directions and miss the point of the passage itself. In fact, the verse has fueled an ongoing battle throughout the centuries between the Trichotomists and the Dichotomists, between those who see humanity as consisting of three parts (body, soul, and spirit) and those who argue for two (body and spirit or soul). Unfortunately for both sides, the Bible itself settled the issue back in Genesis 2. In speaking of the creation of human beings, the Bible plainly teaches that "the Lord God formed man of dust from the ground [the bodily constituents], and breathed into his nostrils the breath [spirit] of life; and man became a living being [soul in the KJV and Hebrew]" (verse 7, NASB). Thus a soul = body + spirit or breath. The Bible furthermore describes death as the reversal of the creation process. In death "the dust [body] returns to the earth as it was, and the spirit [breath] returns to God who gave it" (Eccl. 12:7, RSV). And what about the soul? It is dead, no longer a living being, but in the grave until the resurrection pictured in 1 Thessalonians 4:13-17 and 1 Corinthians 15:51-55, at which time God provides a new body and thus creates a resurrected soul or person. Ernest Best makes that teaching explicit when he observes that "for Paul there is no existence without the body" (Best, p. 243).

Thus the Bible's teaching is not about humans as consisting of essentially two or three elements, but rather of a unity in which all the parts are necessary to have a living being. Thus the reason for the resurrection that stands at the foundation of all hope in 1 Thessalonians 4:13, 18; 5:11.

Having said all those things, we need to realize that 1 Thessalonians is not speaking to the nature of human life. As G. C. Berkouwer points out, "there is no thought in these texts of a scientific description of man's structure" (Berkouwer, p. 210). Leon Morris agrees when he writes that "Paul is not at this point giving a theoretical description of the nature of the human constitution, but engaging in prayer" (Morris, *First and Second*, 1991, p. 182).

The real point of verse 23 is that sanctification is for the whole person. It leaves out no aspect of our lives. No part of us can be held back. We are either living for God or we are not. We must set all our being and powers apart for God. The terms spirit, soul, and body describe the totality of human nature. There is no part of us that God does not want to impact with His sanctifying grace. Thus the second part of verse 23 links up with the first half, which signified that totality with the word "entirely."

Paul's repeated prayer is for entire sanctification so that the

Thessalonian believers might be "preserved ['kept,' RSV] complete and blameless [or 'faultless'] at the coming of our Lord Jesus." Jude 24, which speaks of "him that is able to keep you from falling and to present you faultless before the presence of his glory with exceeding joy" (KJV), presents the same idea. Such faultless ones will be totally dedicated to God in every aspect of their being and will be living lives to His honor and glory.

The perceptive reader will have noted that verse 23 is not the only place in 1 Thessalonians where Paul ties sanctified living to the coming of Christ. The same connection appears in 1 Thessalonians 3:12 and is implied by the judgment language of 4:6. There are at least two reasons for that repeated connection. The first is that the Second Advent has always provided motivation for solid Christian living. People want to "be ready" for that event, a topic that Jesus emphasized again and again in Matthew 24:45 to 25:46. A second reason for the connection is that the Second Advent has an intimate relationship to the concept of a day of reckoning or judgment, in which every person would be rewarded according to their works (Rom. 2:5, 6; Matt. 16:27, 28; Rev. 22:12). While people are certainly justified by grace through faith without works of law (Rom. 3:20-25; Eph. 2:8-10), justification never stands alone in the writings of Paul. Even his great letters on justification (Romans and Galatians) devote their second half to presenting how saved people should behave, which is another way of saying living the sanctified life.

But in the midst of all this sanctified living we need to realize that Christians do not walk the sanctified life on their own. To the contrary, He gives the Holy Spirit for the purpose of empowering our living for Christ and for standing over against the values and ways of the non-Christian culture (1 Thess. 4:8). Paul places God at the center of the sanctification process in 1 Thessalonians 5:24, in which he writes that "the one calling you is faithful, and He will accomplish it." Here we find "the ground of his bold request" (Stott, p. 133). God is not only a caller—He is also a doer. The faithful one, He pledged Himself to carry out what He has promised. Paul's confidence in the Christian life is built upon God's faithfulness. Christians trust not to their own feeble and vacillating strength, but in the power of God who will bring to completion the work that He has begun in His people.

23. Saying Goodbye

1 Thessalonians 5:25-28

25 Brothers, pray for us.
26 Greet all the brothers with a holy kiss. 27 I adjure you by the Lord that this letter be read to all the brothers.
28 The grace of our Lord Jesus Christ be with you.

Is this the "mighty" Paul asking his converts to pray for him? That request ought to help us rethink our picture of apostolic leadership. It is all too easy to picture him as a great man telling others how to make it through the storms of life, but sitting above the tempest himself. Not so! Paul was traveling from place to place in the midst of uncertainty and tension. By the time he writes this letter he had been beaten in Philippi, run out of Thessalonica at night, forced out of Berea, and ignored by the learned ones in Athens (Acts 16:11-17:34). At the time he arrived in Corinth (Acts 18:1), from which he wrote 1 Thessalonians, he was "in weakness and in much fear and trembling" (1 Cor. 2:3, RSV). No wonder he asks for their prayers (1 Thess. 5:25).

Three times in 1 Thessalonians Paul prays for the believers or tells his readers of his prayers for them (1:2; 3:12, 13; 5:23). Now in verse 25 he reverses the roles and asks them to pray for him, a request that Paul will make seven times in his various letters. It flags the truth that ministry is always a two-way street, with struggling sinners found on each side. Paul set forth a similar perspective when he wrote to the believers in Rome that he desired to minister to them in person, but, he added, "don't think I'm not expecting to get something out of this, too! You have as much to give me as I do to you" (Rom. 1:11, Message). We need to view the church not so much as leaders standing above the fray and members in the midst of it, but as a mutual-enhancement society in which every person uplifts each of the others.

> "There is nothing which so directly and powerfully helps a minister of the gospel as the prayers of his congregation". (Denney, p. 259).

Verse 26 commands people to greet each other with "a holy kiss." It has probably been some time since you got a holy kiss at church. Holy kissing has fallen out of style. And for good reason. In the earliest Christian communities members of the same sex exchanged it. But as time went on it broadened to men and women greeting each other with a kiss. That, as we might expect, led to some less than desirable situations. As a result, we find the early church councils passing regulations on the practice.

Today a handshake would be equivalent to a holy kiss. Letting others in the church know that we feel Christian love toward them, it is a display of openness and acceptance. That fraternal greeting was especially crucial in a community such as Thessalonica in which people from various races (including both Jews and Gentiles) and social classes (including slaves and owners) worshipped in the same congregation. It was a sign among the members that they belonged to the one community of those saved in Jesus.

> ## An "Ice-Free" Church
>
> "'Greet one another with a holy kiss' means, Show your Christian love one to another, frankly and heartily . . . . Do not be afraid to break the ice when you come into the church. There should be no ice there to break. Greet your brother or your sister cordially like a Christian; assume and create the atmosphere of home" (Denney, p. 261).

Verse 27 catches the reader off guard. Not because the letter is to be read out loud in the congregation, but because of the forcefulness of the command. I first translated the Greek as "command," but that would have missed an important point. The word is most naturally rendered "I adjure," with the implication that it is more than a mere command. Abraham Malherbe notes that it is a statement of "exceptional earnestness," (Malherbe, *Letters*, p. 342), while Leon Morris indicates that forcefulness by paraphrasing it as "I put you on your oath as Christians" (Morris, *First and Second*, 1959, p. 185). Charles Wanamaker adds his voice, observing that "the forcefulness of this statement is highly unusual, and in fact it is the only instance in Paul's letters where such a charge is laid on the recipients of one of his letters" (Wanamaker, p. 209).

The question that begs an answer, of course, is why the apostle ordered the letter to be read publically in such strong courtroom, oath-like language. We don't know the full answer, but it is probable that he wanted to make sure that everyone in the congregation heard it personally so that there could be no doubt as to exactly what he had said to them on such important topics as living sexually responsible lives (1 Thess. 4:1-8), respecting their local leaders (5:12, 13), working with their hands (4:9-12; 5:14), the situation regarding Christians who had died (4:13-18), and the timing of the Advent (5:1-11). The fact that Paul would again have to treat some of those issues in his second letter to the Thessalonians (see 2 Thess. 2:2; 3:6-15) lends credence to that perspective. He wanted them to hear and understand what he had written.

That the letter would be read orally tells us several things about this early Christian community. For one thing, it informs us that they were following in a tradition long established between God and the Jewish people. In the Old Testament the Lord repeatedly had the law read before the entire congregation (Deut. 31:11; Neh. 8:17, 18). Jesus illustrated the practice in the synagogue (Luke 4:16; cf. Acts 13:27; 15:21) and His disciples did the same in various congregations (Acts 13:14, 15).

The instruction to read the letter publicly also reminds us that the early church belonged to a culture in which many people did not know how to read. In addition, the New Testament did not yet exist. It was an oral culture in which reading aloud the Word of God was the way that He communicated His will to the people.

While those reasons are true, we should also note that the reading of God's Word communally builds community as His people hear and share God's Word together. That is one reason why many congregations today have a reading from both the Old and New Testaments at every worship service. More of such reading is important to the church today. The church needs to hear what the Spirit is saying in a way that PowerPoint and sound bites from the Word of God cannot capture.

We need to note one final point in 1 Thessalonians 5:27. In that verse Paul shifts from the collective "we," which included Timothy and Silvanus, to the first person singular "I." That change probably indicates that the apostle had picked up the pen from the secretary to whom he had been dictating the letter and wrote the last two verses himself. That was certainly the case in 2 Thessalonians 3:17, in which he concludes the letter with "I, Paul, write this greeting with my own hand. This is the mark in every letter of mine; it is the way I write" (RSV). Then he goes on to add the exact same words that he finishes 1 Thessalonians with: "The grace of our Lord Jesus Christ be with you all" (2 Thess. 3:18). The only difference between the two endings is the "all" in 2 Thessalonians.

"Grace" concludes Paul's two letters to Thessalonica, and it forms the focal point of his theology. As such, he begins both First and Second Thessalonians with grace (1 Thess. 1:1; 2 Thess. 1:2) and ends them with the same thought on his mind (1 Thess. 5:28; 2 Thess. 3:18). Being saved by God's gift of grace overwhelmed everything else in Paul's theology and life. For him grace was the beginning and the end of everything meaningful.

Exploring
Second
Thessalonians

Introduction to the
Second Letter to the Thessalonians

While 2 Thessalonians is one of Paul's shorter letters, it is also one of his most forceful and hard-hitting. He had recently written the church in Thessalonica, but since then several of the problems he had dealt with in 1 Thessalonians had become more serious.

Occasion and Purpose of 2 Thessalonians

The immediate occasion for 2 Thessalonians is that the still relatively new Christians in Thessalonica had received a report that the day of the Lord had already arrived (2 Thess. 2:2). According to Paul, they had had thorough instruction on the topic when he had been with them (verse 5). But for some reason it had not registered. As a result, they were now in a state of eschatological excitement that exacerbated already existing problems in their church community. The apostle wrote his second letter primarily to deal with this troubling situation. His basic line of argument in the face of the eschatological crisis was that the day of the Lord could not come until the "man of lawlessness" who takes to himself the prerogatives and honors of God had arisen (verses 3, 4).

To make matters worse, those whom Paul had rebuked in his first letter because of their decision not to work due to the nearness of the Second Advent (1 Thess. 4:9-12; 5:14) apparently had taken the information that the day of the Lord had already arrived as a vindication of their position. The result was an entrenched no-work attitude that the apostle's second letter addressed in strong confrontational tones (2 Thess. 3:6-14). If they won't work, he thundered, let them starve (verse 10). Again, if they refused to obey, the congregation was to refuse to fellowship with them. Hopefully their sense of shame and lack of acceptance would wake them up from their folly (verses 14, 15).

Inextricably intertwined with the day of the Lord crisis within the church was the fact that the persecution the new believers had been undergoing from the non-Christian community had intensified (2 Thess. 1:5). That problem brought from Paul an explicit statement about judgment to come (verses 6-10) at which time God would make things right by honoring His saints (verse 10) and destroying those who fought against the gospel (verses 6-9). Thus a second purpose of 2 Thessalonians was to reassure believers and encourage them to hold on in the face of persecution and the delay of the Advent.

Second Thessalonians is a forceful letter that shows Paul near the height of his aggressiveness. But in the face of that assertiveness we must remember that he composed it to meet an urgent crisis that threatened to destroy the new church from both the outside and the inside. Strong language was needed in the face of imminent disaster.

Major Themes in 2 Thessalonians

All of the significant themes found in 1 Thessalonians now reappear in the second letter. Thus the role of God as sovereign and Jesus as Lord, the Second Advent, responsible holy living, and positive encouragement in pastoral ministry all have a significant place in 2 Thessalonians. However, the second letter will significantly expand the apostle's treatment on two of those topics and add one alluded to in 1 Thessalonians but not developed. Beyond that, 2 Thessalonians will reinforce two subthemes also present in the first letter.

1. *The man of lawlessness.* The man of lawlessness is the central doctrinal teaching in 2 Thessalonians. Paul notes that the Second Advent will not take place until he is fully revealed. He will exalt himself, put himself in the place of God, work signs and wonders, but finally be destroyed at the coming of the Lord (2 Thess. 2:3, 4, 9, 8). M. C. Tenney points out that the person's identity "has been a standing puzzle to exegetes and commentators because the prophecy has never been completely fulfilled" (Tenney, in Bromiley, *International*, vol. 4, p. 834).

In this connection, it is important to note that the teachings in 2 Thessalonians on the Second Advent are in actuality an extension of what Paul had earlier presented in 1 Thessalonians 4:13-5:11. Thus the second letter fills in blanks in Paul's eschatological teaching that would have been lost to us if he had never written it.

2. *God's judgment.* Second Thessalonians mentions the word "judgment" only one time (2 Thess. 1:5), but the concept of divine judgment pervades the letter. Paul depicts judgment as coming in two flavors. On the one hand is the glorification of the saints at the Second Advent (verses 5, 10). And on the other hand is the utter destruction of those who persecute God's people and who "do not obey the gospel of our Lord Jesus" (verses 6-9, RSV). That negative aspect of divine judgment appears a second time in this short letter in chapter 2, in which we find divine destruction of the man of lawlessness (2 Thess. 2:8). Paul's judgment language in 2 Thessalonians finds few parallels in terms of vividness as he expounds upon what the book of Revelation refers to as the "wrath of the Lamb" (Rev. 6:16).

3. *Responsible living while waiting for the Advent.* Paul's treatment of the topic in 2 Thessalonians is more restricted than in his first letter, in which he dealt with sexual purity (1 Thess. 4:1-8), respecting church leaders (5:12, 13), general Christian behavior (5:15-22), and the necessity of useful labor while waiting for the Lord (4:9-12; 5:14). By way of comparison, 2 Thessalonians treats responsible living almost exclusively in terms of believers continuing to work while waiting for the Lord (3:6-14). Here we have an issue that was problematic when Paul had first written, but had grown much worse in the interval. It was undoubtedly causing tension in the church itself as those who still labored had to support nonworking individuals. In addition, it may have been causing disrespect from the non-Christian community and thus exacerbating already inflamed tensions between the two groups.

4. *Christian perseverance.* A fourth theme evident in 2 Thessalonians is the need for Christians to remain steadfast in the face of persecution. That teaching has no major didactic section in the epistle, but it is raised explicitly in 2 Thessalonians 1:4 and undergirds the letter's prayers and exhortations (2 Thess. 1:3, 4, 11, 12; 2:13-17; 3:1-5).

5. *Holding to the apostolic teachings.* Another topic that weaves through-

out 2 Thessalonians is the need to "stand firm and hold to the traditions which you were taught, either by our words or by a letter from us" (2 Thess. 2:15). Part of the problem that stimulated the need for a second letter was that the Thessalonians had not remembered what Paul had taught them earlier (verse 5). Apostolic authority is a major concern in both of the Thessalonian letters.

Structure and Outline of 2 Thessalonians

Like 1 Thessalonians, 2 Thessalonians is easy to outline. It has a brief introduction (1:1, 2), a body divided into personal concerns (1:3-12) and instruction and exhortation (2:1-3:15), and a conclusion (3:16-18). One point of structural interest is that the two letters have exactly the same structural formats. The following outline represents the framework of Paul's second letter to the Thessalonians:

I. Greetings (1:1, 2)
II. Personal matters (1:3-12)
   A. Thanksgiving for the Thessalonians (1:3, 4)
   B. Encouragement to endure (1:5-10)
   C. Prayer for the Thessalonians (1:11, 12)
III. Instruction and Exhortation (2:1-3:15)
   A. Instruction about events to precede the day of the Lord (2:1-12)
   B. Thanksgiving that God had called the Thessalonian believers and an encouragement for them to stand fast (2:13-15)
   C. Prayer for the Thessalonians (2:16, 17)
   D. Exhortation for the Thessalonians to pray for Paul and his colleagues and a prayer for them (3:1-5)
   E. Exhortation to labor or suffer church discipline (3:6-15)
IV. Conclusion (3:16-18)

2 Thessalonians' Relevance for the Twenty-first Century

A central aspect in 2 Thessalonians' relevance in our day is its highlighting of end-time events related to the rise of "the man of lawlessness" and their implications. Since Jesus told His disciples to watch and be ready (Matt. 24:42), the teachings of 2 Thessalonians 2:1-11 are a necessary aspect of understanding as a troubled world awaits "the day of the Lord."

Also significant in this short letter is the counsel to persevere in the face of difficulty. The fact that God will correct all injustices when Christ returns is an encouragement to His followers as they struggle through difficult situations often brought about because of their Christian beliefs and their dedication to live them out in a less than understanding or sympathetic world.

A final aspect of relevance is the admonition to remember the teachings of the apostles (2 Thess. 2:15), which we now have recorded in our Bibles. The alternative is to be led astray by those who claim to have a word from the Lord, but who are out of harmony with apostolic teaching (see 2 Thess. 2:2). We can thank God daily for His guidance in the Bible.

List of Works Cited

(See introduction to 1 Thessalonians.)

Part I

Personal Matters

2 Thessalonians 1:1-12

1. Encouraging Words to a Faithful Church

2 Thessalonians 1:1-4

> ¹*Paul and Silvanus and Timothy,*
>
> *To the church of the Thessalonians in God our Father and the Lord Jesus Christ.*
>
> ²*Grace to you and peace from the Father and the Lord Jesus Christ.*
>
> ³*We are bound to thank God always concerning you, brothers, as is fitting, because your faith is growing abundantly and the love of every one of you toward one another is increasing.*
>
> ⁴*Therefore we ourselves boast of you among the churches of God for your perseverance and faith in all of your persecutions and the afflictions which you are enduring.*

The greeting in verses 1 and 2 is almost an exact replica of that in 1 Thessalonians 1:1, 2. As a result, I have not provided a separate section for it in 2 Thessalonians since readers already have an exposition in 1 Thessalonians.

While the wording of the two greetings is nearly exact, 2 Thessalonians does make two significant additions. First, whereas the initial letter greets "the church of the Thessalonians in God *the* Father," this one calls Him "our Father." That shift may be small, but it is meaningful. It implies that God for these new believers is not merely some impersonal "other," but the Deity with whom these converted pagans now have an intimate relationship. But the plural "our" has not only a vertical relationship to God as Father but also a horizontal dimension implying that the new believers belong to the family of God. They were not alone in either their troubles or their faith.

The second change in the greeting of 2 Thessalonians is that after "grace to you and peace" the apostle adds "from the Father and the Lord Jesus Christ" (verse 2), thereby specifying the source of their blessing. Those added words became Paul's standard greeting, found in all of his letters except 1 Thessalonians and Colossians. The apostle desired to constantly remind his readers of the divine origin of the grace and peace that meant so much to them in their daily lives. Divine "grace and peace" had special significance to the believers in Thessalonica, who faced persecution and affliction (2 Thess. 1:4). Later in the letter Paul prays, "may our Lord Jesus Christ Himself and God our Father, who loved us and has given us eternal comfort and good hope through grace, comfort your hearts and establish them in every good work" (2 Thess. 2:16, 17). It was God's grace, and that grace only, that provided them with hope and peace in a social context of rejection and violence. Meanwhile, the focal point of hope in both Thessalonian letters is the second coming of Jesus. Hope for those harried Christians was not an abstraction but a belief that made their life meaningful. Those of us who live in more comfortable circumstances (for the present at least) need to get our perspective corrected. Too often our hope in the wrong things crowds out the only hope that is truly meaningful.

After the greeting, the rest of 2 Thessalonians 1 falls into three sections:

1. a thanksgiving for God's grace in their lives (verses 3, 4),

2. encouragement for continued endurance (verses 5–10a), and

3. a prayer for God's power (verses 11, 12).

"We are bound to thank God always concerning you." Here we have not merely a routine appreciation but a heartfelt word of gratitude that expresses a strong sense of obligation that we can understand only as it relates to the difficult situation in which the Thessalonians have been existing. The very quality of their dynamic faith and love in that context compels the apostle to thank God for their faithfulness. And their perseverance is especially meaningful to him since he had feared that their afflictions might overcome them and cause such new believers to give up Christianity (1 Thess. 3:1-5). Paul had been overjoyed and thankful for their steadfastness when he had received Timothy's report of their continuing faith and faithfulness (1 Thess. 3:6-9).

The apostle is still thankful for that faithful congregation. But now in

2 Thessalonians he has even more to be appreciative about. That is the topic of 2 Thessalonians 1:3. The Thessalonian Christians have not only remained faithful in the midst of difficult circumstances, but their "faith is growing abundantly and the love of every one of you toward one another is increasing."

As with 1 Thessalonians, the second letter begins with an expression of heartfelt thanksgiving to God for His blessing on the believers in Thessalonica. While there are many similarities between the thanksgivings in the two letters, we also observe some significant differences. We have already noted the first of them. While in his initial epistle Paul simply stated that "we give thanks to God always for all of you" (1 Thess. 1:2), his second letter emphasizes the obligatory nature ("we are bound") of that thankfulness. That stronger language reflects the apostle's wonder and profound appreciation of the fact that their spiritual growth had not merely remained constant but had flourished in spite of their ongoing persecution.

It is in that dynamic, accelerating change in their religious experience that we find the second change in the apostle's expression of gratitude compared to the first letter. That former one had expressed thankfulness for their "work of faith and labor of love and steadfastness of hope" (1 Thess. 1:3), but this one speaks of faith "growing abundantly" and love "increasing." Here we find a dynamic word combination that expresses exuberant growth—"to grow over and beyond" what is expected (Rogers, p. 482). It is the "figure of the tree of faith growing above (*huper*) measure" (Robertson, vol. 4, p. 41). Such is the explosive nature of their faith.

Verse 3 reflects the fact that their love is "increasing." In his first letter the apostle had urged the Thessalonians to exhibit love toward each other "more and more" (1 Thess. 4:10) and had prayed that their love to one another might "increase and overflow" (1 Thess. 3:12). His thankfulness in 2 Thessalonians for their actively "increasing" love represents an answer to his earlier prayer. They took something they had been doing fairly well and did it even better.

Here we need to stop and meditate on the dynamic words Paul employs in his thankfulness. They are living words—faith "growing abundantly" and love for one another "increasing." Both are in the present tense indicating ongoing growth that is continuing to develop from the past into the future. We need to capture that dynamism in our personal

Christian experience. John Stott points out that too many people treat faith in a static way as something they have or don't have. Thus they complain, saying "'I've lost my faith' like 'I've lost my spectacles,' as if it were a commodity." But faith, he adds, "is a relationship of trust in God, and like all relationships is a living, dynamic, growing thing." Love, likewise, "is a living relationship, whose growth we can take steps to nurture" (Stott, p. 144).

A third change from the thankfulness section of 1 Thessalonians is the absence of the word "hope" in the second letter. But just because the word is missing does not mean that the epistle lacks the concept of hope. To the contrary, we find the "steadfastness of hope" (1 Thess. 1:3) implied in 2 Thessalonians 1:4, which speaks of "your perseverance and faith in all of your persecutions and . . . afflictions." Their hope was what was sustaining them in those troublesome times.

That thought brings me to the word that I translated as "perseverance." Although *hypomonē* is often rendered as "patience" or "endurance," the word does not simply mean waiting with "resignation," but "waiting" with blazing hope. "It is not the patience which grimly waits for the end, but the patience which radiantly hopes for the dawn" (Rogers, 482). "As distinct from patience, it has the active significance of energetic . . . resistance" (Bromiley, *Theological*, p. 582). Revelation 14:12 employs the word to express the attitude of those who are experiencing the last great conflict at the end of time and look with profound hope for the return of their Lord (verses 14–20). Paul boasts of the Thessalonians to other churches that they possess a persevering hope that not only patiently endures suffering but informs and energizes their entire lives.

> ## Hypomonē
>
> "Patience, endurance. The word indicates a remaining under, i.e., a bearing up under difficult circumstances. It is the spirit which can bear things, not simply with resignation but with blazing hope. It is not the patience which grimly waits for the end, but the patience which radiantly hopes for the dawn" (Rogers, 482).

A final thing that we should note about the thankfulness section in 2 Thessalonians as compared to the first letter is that it adds a few words about Paul's boasting about the "perseverance and faith" of the Thessalonians to other churches (2 Thess. 1:4). He obviously did it to encourage other churches—"Look at how those Thessalonians are holding up in difficult circumstances." But he may also have written of such boasting to the Thessalonians to encourage them in the shame they may have been experiencing as a persecuted group of social outcasts. In effect, he is saying that though Thessalonian society may have ostracized them, that they were being upheld as models in Christian communities everywhere. Thus they had significance in the family of God. In parting, we should note that Paul was not boasting so much about their accomplishments but about what God had done in them. For that reality Paul could praise God while at the same time letting them know that they were an encouragement to him.

We can all thank God that He is the kind of Father whom we can hope and trust in. It is an understanding of that sort of God that provides a foundation for that hope and faith that leads to daily perseverance in spiritual things.

2. Encouraging Words on God's Justice

2 Thessalonians 1:5-10

[5]*Here is evidence of the righteous judgment of God, that you will be declared worthy of the kingdom of God, for which you are also suffering.* [6]*For indeed it is just for God to repay with affliction those who afflict you,* [7]*and to give rest to those being afflicted, and to us also, when the Lord Jesus will be revealed from heaven with His mighty angels in flaming fire,* [8]*inflicting punishment upon those who do not know God and upon those not obeying the gospel of our Lord Jesus.* [9]*They will pay the penalty of eternal destruction, away from the presence of the Lord and from the glory of His might,* [10]*when He comes to be glorified in His saints on that day, and to be marveled at by all those who have believed—because our testimony to you was believed.*

Have you ever suffered for doing good? It is bad enough to experience it because of bad actions, but it is worse to endure it for doing good things. That was the situation of the Thessalonians who faced persecution because they had become Christians.

"Where is the justice in this?" their hearts must have cried out. But the situation was nothing new. The psalmist anguished over the fact that the wicked flourished while the righteous suffered. And the problem is still with us in the twenty-first century. "Why doesn't God do something?" is the perpetual question asked by those suffering unjustly. The answer is that He will do something—but not yet.

Second Thessalonians 1:5-10 addresses these questions and in the process provides us with crucial information as we begin to think about the theology of suffering. Paul's answer consists of two parts: (1) an application of the justice of God to the present situation of the Thessalonians (verse 5), and (2) God's justice in making all things right at the second coming of Jesus (verses 6-10). Before examining those two aspects of divine justice, we need to remember that the apostle is not writing an abstract argument on the theory of suffering and justice, but is reaching out in his letter to a group of believers who need encouragement to endure their affliction.

The first part of Paul's presentation is his statement that their present sufferings (highlighted in verse 4) are "evidence of the righteous judgment of God" and are part of the process by which they will "be declared worthy of the kingdom of God" (verse 5). That sounds like strange logic to our twenty-firstcentury minds. After all, for most of us suffering seems to be a denial of God's presence in our lives rather than evidence of it. But such was not the thinking of the writers of the New Testament. While we think of suffering as nothing but evil, the New Testament presents it as a part of the providence of God as He works out our salvation.

In 2 Thessalonians 1:5 Paul presents a lesson that his first readers desperately needed to hear—that the persecution raging against them was not a sign of their rejection by God, but a symbol of their acceptance by Him. He would use it to develop them for His kingdom.

That insight is also important to those of us living 2,000 years later. It is all too easy to think that God has deserted us. Not so! the apostle tells us. That may be the time that He is closest to us as we surrender to His transforming grace in His ongoing work of making us into citizens of His kingdom.

But some of us modern Christians are tempted to worry that something must be wrong with our Christian experience if we are not suffering enough. Paul's counsel to such individuals would probably be not to get too concerned. Rejoice and build a connection with God in your peaceful times, because each of us will have crises enough down the track. It may be a minor problem like an illness or a major one such as a death in the family, a crippling automobile accident, or an unjust financial crisis shoving us into bankruptcy, but God can use each and every one of them to develop Christian character. He lets no opportunity pass in the development of His people for eternity. Our lives may be peaceful in the present due to the wide acceptance of general Christianity in many cultures, but the time will come, according to 2 Thessalonians 2 and Revelation 13, when the "man of lawlessness" will gain full power and provide us with all sorts of opportunities to grow in grace. In the meantime, we have a wonderful opportunity to learn to know how to walk with the Lord of grace and to understand His Word to the church in both times of peace and moments of suffering and persecution.

A New Testament View of Suffering

- "We rejoice in our sufferings, knowing that suffering produces endurance, and endurance produces character, and character produces hope, and hope does not disappoint us, because God's love has been poured into our hearts through the Holy Spirit which has been given to us" (Rom. 5:3-5, RSV).

- In response to the harassment of Satan in his own life, Paul could write of a God who said, "My grace is sufficient for you, for my power is made perfect in weakness." To that proclamation the apostle responded, "I will all the more gladly boast of my weaknesses, that the power of Christ may rest upon me. For the sake of Christ, then, I am content with weaknesses, insults, hardships, persecutions, and calamities; for when I am weak, then I am strong" (2 Cor. 12:9, 10, RSV).

- With those Pauline passages in mind we can begin to understand Jesus better when He said, "Blessed are those who are persecuted for righteousness' sake, for theirs is the kingdom of heaven" (Matt. 5:10, RSV).

The second aspect of God's justice developed in 2 Thessalonians 1 treats His making all things right at the Second Advent through the judgment of those who rebel in one way or another against God. Paul provided his teaching on the topic in verses 6–10 to encourage the Thessalonian believers who were experiencing persecution. As Gene Green puts it, the passage supplies "them with an eschatological perspective that will enable them to evaluate their present situation rightly" (Green, p. 287). Their invisible God may seem insignificant compared with the outward beauty of the pagan temples, but the invisible will become overwhelmingly visible when He returns in glory with a multitude of angels. The Christian God might appear helpless and powerless in a world in which the enemies of the faith have abundant power, but that power will be as nothing compared to that of the returning Christ. The believers were suffering for their faith from the oppressors, but when Christ returns He will make all things right in divine judgment. Then those who abuse power will meet with "eternal destruction" (verse 9). In short, there is hope for the future, so be faithful until that time. Such was Paul's encouragement to the suffering Thessalonians.

While the topic of the final judgment of the wicked may have brought comfort to those early believers in their stressed-out state of existence, it brings a vigorous rejection from many modern people who live, so to speak, "in palaces of ease." The God of love, they claim, wouldn't do such a thing. Wouldn't He? Is it better for Him just to sit eternally on His hands and do nothing as a ceaseless flow of children die of hunger and the millions sold into sex slavery vanish into disease and death while the wealthy sellers pocket the money? Or should the God of love and justice in some way "force" everyone to love Him and become good?

Not so, says the Bible from one end to the other. God in His love will terminate the mess that we call world history at the Second Advent. To reject the teaching of the final judgment is not merely to avoid 2 Thessalonians 1:6-10, but to put aside the teachings of Jesus on the topic (Matt. 7:19; 10:28; 25:46) and the entire book of Revelation (see, e.g., chapters 19 and 20). The Bible is consistently clear on the subject. God at the close of time will in His love and justice make things right. Second Thessalonians 1:6, 7 points out that God's judgment has two edges. Those who afflict will be afflicted (verse 6), and those afflicted will receive heavenly "rest" (verse 7, cf. Heb. 4:9).

The agent of judgment is none other than the Lord Jesus, for whom His people have given up so much to follow. He will return (1) from heaven, (2) with His angels, (3) in flaming fire (verse 7; cf. 1 Thess. 4:14-17; Matt. 24:30, 31; Rev. 19). The "flaming fire" points to both His divine glory (Ex. 3:2; Isa. 66:15; Rev. 1:13-15) and the form of the punishment in verse 8 to those who refuse the knowledge of God (cf. Rom. 1:28) and reject living by that law of love that undergirds the ethical message of Jesus (Matt. 22:36-40).

As in most cases in the Bible, 2 Thessalonians has no problem with the issue of end-time rewards. The eventual punishment of the oppressors will be "eternal destruction" (2 Thess. 1:9), while those who have given so much for Christ will find deliverance.

The concept of "eternal destruction" has elicited a variation of responses. Green, for example, writes that "the apostle by no means implies that those who have rejected God will be annihilated eternally, a notion that appears to take the edge off the severity of divine judgment." He sees the punishment as ongoing. It will not end (Green, p. 292). Such an argument, although held by many, says something about the character of a deity who could punish people throughout the ceaseless ages of eternity.

The alternative is to understand "eternal destruction" as having eternal results, an idea represented in the word *olethros*, which can be rendered as either "death" or "destruction" (Bauer, p. 702; Thayer, p. 443). As a result, we could translate the phrase as "eternal death," an understanding reflected in Revelation 20:14, 15 as the "second death." "Eternal destruction" is the opposite of eternal life (see Rom. 6:23) and does not represent endless torment, but rather a destruction that lasts forever (see also Rev. 20:9, Mal. 4:1, 3; Matt. 10:28). That understanding lines up with the fact that only the righteous receive immortality when Christ returns (1 Cor. 15:51-54; see remarks on 1 Thess. 4:14). Thus their "eternal life" lasts throughout the ceaseless ages. On the other hand, those who reject the rule of God are not given immortality. As a result, they cannot exist in perpetual punishment, but suffer "eternal destruction" or "eternal death" or "the second death." Jesus taught the same thing when He referred to killing the soul (total person) as its eternal destruction (Matt. 10:28). And the prophet Malachi described the fate of the wicked as total obliteration (Mal. 4:1, 3).

By way of contrast, the ultimate reward of those who have accepted

God's salvation in Christ is life everlasting in the presence of their Savior (see Rev. 21; 22). Second Thessalonians 1:6-10 closes with the teaching that at the end of time Christ will "be glorified in His saints" and "be marveled at by all those who have believed" (verse 10). Throughout eternity God's people will have nothing but praise for Him. With that in mind, those of us in the twenty-first century, like the Thessalonians of old, need to "hang on" to our faith in the Christ who will return again and make all things right "on that day" (verse 10).

3. Prayerful Words

2 Thessalonians 1:11, 12
> *[11]With this in mind also we always pray concerning you, that our God will count you worthy of your calling, and fulfill every desire for goodness and the work of faith with [His] power, [12]so that the name of our Lord Jesus may be glorified in you, and you in Him, according to the grace of our God and Lord, Jesus Christ.*

With this in mind" refers us back to Paul's thanksgiving for, and encouragement of, the Thessalonian believers in verses 3-10. He has just written about coming glory and deliverance. But he is quite aware of the fact that they are still only midcourse in their Christian journey. They stand between their positive response to the calling of God to join Christ and His future coming "from heaven" in "flaming fire" with His angels (1:7). The apostle well recognizes the challenge that will continue to confront them as they live out their Christianity in a world hostile to their beliefs and values. He knows that they can never succeed in their own strength. So he prays for these struggling believers that they might take hold of the power of God so that when Jesus returns His name will be glorified through them.

His prayer has two petitions. The first is that they will be counted worthy of their calling (verse 11). Here the Revised Standard Version has "may make you worthy of his call." That is a permissible translation, but is ruled out by Paul's overall theology. He is clear that "there is no possibility of our establishing or accumulating merit in such a way as to deserve God's favour" (Stott, p. 150). The gospel is always one of grace and never one of our worthiness. Christians are called by grace in a state of unworthiness (Gal. 1:13-15) and will be sustained by grace throughout their lives. They are "counted" worthy, not "made" worthy. Our standing before God never is on the basis of our own merits.

On the other hand, the Lord does not expect us to live unworthily. To the contrary, Paul begs us "to lead a life worthy of the calling to which [we] have been called" (Eph. 4:1, RSV). As the apostle so often notes, Christianity is a "walk" with Jesus in the way of righteousness. People's lives are transformed when they come to Jesus (Rom. 12:2). Thereafter they "walk in the newness of life" in the ways of God and refuse to let sin reign in their lives (Rom. 6:4, 12, RSV).

Those thoughts bring us to Paul's second petition in 2 Thessalonians 1:11—that God will "fulfill every desire for goodness and the work of faith with [His] power." My translation closely follows the Greek text which, while accurate, tends to mute the forcefulness of the statement. The freer rendering of the Good News Translation helps us clarify the point: "May he fulfill by his power all your desire for goodness and complete your work of faith." Phillips is also helpful: "that God . . . by his power may fulfil all your good intentions and every effort of faith."

We need to emphasize at least two things in this petition. First, Christians should have a "desire for goodness" and "works of faith." While God calls them in an unworthy state, He does not intend that they remain in the same condition in which He found them. Their faith will make a difference in their lives. Leon Morris reminds us that "faith is not simply an intellectual attitude that does nothing. Faith is always busy. A true faith will clothe itself in works. So Paul prays that his friends will produce in their lives the works that spring from faith" (Morris, *First and Second*, 1991, pp. 209, 210). Paul effectually illustrates that truth in his great saved-by-grace book of Romans, which is bracketed by the words "obedience of faith" in both its introduction and conclusion (Rom. 1:5; 16:26). Faith always leads to obedience. But that obedience is always in the context of saving faith.

A second point that he makes clear in the second petition of verse 11 is that the power to live the life of goodness and do works of faith comes from God. We hear a lot about forgiving and justifying grace, but here the apostle speaks about God's gift of empowering grace—the grace that enables converted Christians to walk with Jesus. That fact harmonizes with Paul's teaching on "the obedience of faith" and "the work of faith." He always rejects obedience and works performed outside of a faith relationship to God. The difference is the quality of the power. Under our own power we are doomed to failure. But under the empowerment of the Holy Spirit as God's children we can find victory.

The two petitions of 2 Thessalonians 1:11, which deal with being counted worthy and being empowered by God to live the work of faith, come together in what we might think of as the verse's future implications, represented by God's final evaluation of a Christian's conduct at the end of time. Paul raised that issue in Romans 2 when he pointed to the day of "God's righteous judgment," in which "he will render to every man according to his works" (verses 5, 6, RSV). Along that line, D.E.H. Whiteley notes that "God most certainly does not disregard moral qualities at the Last Day, as we can see from 2 Cor. 5:10 ('For we must all appear before the judgement seat of Christ, so that each one may receive good or evil according to what he has done in the body')" (Whiteley, p. 95). Thus being counted worthy has both present and future implications.

Second Thessalonians 1:12 explains the purpose of the progress in the believers' lives that Paul and his colleagues have been praying for— that His name might be glorified in them and that they might be glorified in Him. Please note that the primary emphasis is on the honor and glorifi-

The Flavors of Grace

Grace comes in several varieties. Four of them are:

1. Calling grace, which wakes up each of us to our lost condition and impels us toward Christ.
2. Forgiving and justifying grace, which saves us from the penalty of sin.
3. Sanctifying grace, which saves from the dominating power of sin in our lives and empowers us to walk with Jesus as we grow in grace.
4. Glorifying grace, which at the end of time will transform God's followers from mortal to immortal and from corruptible to incorruptible (see 1 Cor. 15:51-54) and saves us from the presence of sin.

cation of God rather than that of His followers. There is a reason for that. Namely, that they have nothing to boast of in themselves. Before God found them they were self-centered and lost in the maze of sin in all its varieties. It was only through the grace of God that they found health, healing, and salvation. Thus it is God who makes the difference. As a result, in the last day He will be "glorified in His saints" (2 Thess. 1:10, 12). But, verse 12 indicates, the process is reciprocal. God will glorify them at the end of time. Their glory comes from being "in Him." At that point in verse 12 Paul again raises the issue of grace, because it is grace that supplies their salvation and hope all the way from their calling as Christians to their glorification.

The final point in verse 12 is that human glorification comes from "our God and Lord, Jesus Christ" (cf. NIV footnote to verse 12). Another possible translation (the one chosen by most versions) is "our God and the Lord Jesus Christ" (RSV, NASB). I translated the phrase as "our God and Lord, Jesus Christ" because the definite article before "Lord" is not in the Greek. The implication is that Paul is acknowledging Jesus as God in the text. That identification is not out of harmony with the overall theology of the Thessalonian correspondence, which grants Jesus many of the prerogatives of God. Beyond that, Titus 2:13 refers to "our great God and Savior Jesus Christ" (RSV), and the New Testament ascribes the title "God" to Jesus in several places (see, e.g., John 1:1; 20:28; Heb. 1:8, 9; 1 John 5:20).

Having said that, the rendering of the Greek as "our God and the Lord Jesus Christ" is also permissible. In that case, verse 12 is not calling Jesus God, but rather placing Him as equal to God the Father. And, of course, that equality implies Christ's divinity, which as we saw above, the New Testament plainly teaches.

In the long run, both translations of verse 12 lead to the same place. Our salvation results from the grace of God. He is the one that Paul is praying to for his friends in Thessalonica. And He is the one who even today counts us worthy and empowers us to live the life of faith.

Part II

Instructional Matters

2 Thessalonians 2:1-17

4. Instruction Regarding the Great Apostasy

2 Thessalonians 2:1-8

¹Now we request you, brothers, with regard to the coming of our Lord Jesus Christ and our gathering together to Him, ²that you be not quickly shaken in your mind, or be alarmed either by a spirit or by a verbal communication or by a letter, as if from us, to the effect that the day of the Lord has come. ³Let no one deceive you in any way, because it will not come until the apostasy comes first and the man of lawlessness is revealed, the son of destruction, ⁴who opposes and exalts himself above every so-called god or object of worship, so that he takes his seat in the temple of God, proclaiming himself to be God. ⁵Do you not remember that while I was still with you, I was telling you these things? ⁶And you know what is restraining him now, so that he may be revealed in his own time. ⁷For the mystery of lawlessness is working already; only the one now restraining it will do so until he is taken out of the way. ⁸And then the lawless one will be revealed, whom the Lord will destroy by the breath of His mouth and will bring to an end by the appearance of His coming.

With 2 Thessalonians 2:1-12 we have come to what one commentator calls "the very heart of the epistle" (Hiebert, p. 299). While that is true, it has been a difficult passage for scholars to reach agreement on. Albert Barnes wrote more than a century ago that "there is scarcely any passage of the New Testament which has given occasion to greater diversity of opinion than this" (Barnes, p. 79). William Neil describes these verses as "the weirdest piece of writing in all the epistles" (Neil, *St. Paul's Epistle,* p. 132).

John Stott adds his bit to the chorus of interesting remarks by noting that students of the passage should remember the "need for humility. Church history is littered with incautious, self-confident but mistaken attempts to find in Paul's text a reference to some contemporary person or event. Let this be a warning to us to be more cautious and tentative than some others have been." He balances that caution by claiming that "we have no liberty to abandon the [interpretive] task as hopeless, for 2 Thessalonians 2 is an important part of Scripture, which has been written and preserved for the church's instruction" (Stott, pp. 161, 162).

The occasion for Paul's penning 2 Thessalonians 2:1-8 involved further perplexity among the Thessalonians regarding the Second Advent. Their confusion that stimulated his first letter had to do with both the problem of dying believers (1 Thess. 4:13-18) and the timing of the eschaton (1 Thess. 5:1-11). The apostle had apparently explained the first issue to their satisfaction, but they were still bewildered regarding the second. More specifically, some had accepted the teaching that the Second Coming had already taken place (2 Thess. 2:2). That baffled the apostle because he had thoroughly instructed them on the topic when he first evangelized them (verse 5). Beyond that, he had explicitly written to them of the public, earth-shaking nature of the event in his first letter (see 1 Thess. 4:16, 17).

How had they become confused? Paul isn't certain, but in 2 Thessalonians 2:2 he tells them in no uncertain terms that they were not to become disturbed "by a spirit or by a verbal communication or by a letter" purporting to be from the apostolic team and claiming that Christ had already arrived. A summary of Paul's solution to the topic was for them to remember what he had already taught them on the topic (verse 5), including the fact that the Second Advent could not take place until certain events transpired (verses 3, 4).

Here we need to highlight one refrain that runs throughout both Thessalonian letters. Namely, that the basis for Christian belief is what the apostolic team had taught them in the beginning (1 Thess. 1:5; 2:1, 2, 5, 11; 3:3, 4; 4:2; 5:2; 2 Thess. 3:7). That teaching runs throughout the New Testament (see, e.g., 1 John 2:24; Titus 1:9; Jude 3). As a result, the apostolic teaching preserved in the New Testament is to be the basis of all Christian doctrine and practice. It must also be the test for all other teachings that come to Christians.

Second Thessalonians 2:2 indicates that the Thessalonian congregation had already messed up on that point in at least one of three ways. Paul wasn't sure which one was the culprit, so he mentions all of them. First, he points out that they may have gotten their false information through "a spirit," meaning a spiritual gift. We know from the first letter that the gift of prophecy was an issue in the congregation. The apostle had already cautioned them not to despise such teachers, but to test them and accept only that which proved to be true (1 Thess. 5:19-21). The second possible venue for the false teaching was an oral communication. Along that line, we know from other New Testament letters that traveling preachers circulated among the churches promoting false teachings (2 John 7; 2 Tim. 2:17, 18). Alternately, the false information may have come through a letter, one purporting to have been written by Paul himself. It was in order to guard against such counterfeits that the apostle personally signed his letters (2 Thess. 3:17).

No matter how they got the false teaching, he implies, they should have examined it in light of what he had taught them earlier (2 Thess. 2:5). But since they didn't take that precaution, or perhaps because they had failed to understand his teaching or had forgotten it, he presents some of it again beginning in verse 3. Unfortunately, he only touches the highlights of his earlier teaching. As a result, later interpreters, not having the complete picture, have had a great deal of difficulty in coming to agreement on the full implications of the text. But the general outline is clear enough.

> **Good Advice for Contemporary Christians**
>
> "The Thessalonians had accepted the content of the false teaching merely because of the means by which it came to them. We might caution modern Christians to understand that the message of every radio or television preacher, or even every person who stands behind a pulpit, needs to be examined through the lens of apostolic teaching as contained in Scripture" (Green, pp. 304, 305).

Verse 3 informs us that two things must happen before the Second Advent: (1) "the apostasy" must take place, and (2) "the man of lawlessness" must be revealed. The apostasy described is of a religious nature rather than being a revolt from government. And the presence of the definite article ("*the* apostasy") indicates that he refers to a specific apostasy, something that the apostle had earlier explained to his readers. Hints at future apostasy surface throughout the New Testament. Paul, for example, predicts one that would begin within the church by "men speaking perverse things, to draw away the disciples after them" (Acts 20:30, RSV). Peter and Jude blast those who have forsaken apostolic teachings (2 Peter 2:1, 12-22; Jude 4, 10-13). John testifies that by the time of his writing many antichrists had come (1 John 2:18). And Jesus Himself had taught that false prophets would arise and lead many astray (Matt. 24:24).

Paul does not identify "the man of lawlessness" by name, but rather by characteristics. He mentions five. First, the lawless one was already working at the time Paul wrote 2 Thessalonians (verse 7). That fact agrees with what we discovered about apostasy in the previous paragraph. Second, he is lawless, or in opposition to law. Presumably that implies that he will deny the validity of God's moral law.

Third, he will be in opposition to God Himself. Specifically, he exalts himself above God and "takes his seat in the temple of God, proclaiming himself to be God" (verse 4). Here we find a state of mind linked in the Old Testament to Satan, personified in Isaiah 14 as the king of Babylon, who says in his heart, "I will ascend to heaven; . . . I will make myself like the Most High" (verses 13, 14, RSV). Again, Ezekiel 28 personifies Satan as the king of Tyre who announces, "I am a god, I sit in the seat of the gods" (verse 2, see also verses 13-17). In such texts we find the Old Testament root of the New Testament teaching on the antichrist.

The word "antichrist" has two meanings: (1) against Christ and (2) in place of Christ. Second Thessalonians 2 implies both meanings even though the word "antichrist" is not in the passage. It appears that the power undergirding the several "antichrists" (1 John 2:18) in the New Testament is none other than Satan himself, whose very name means "adversary." He is the ultimate lawless one, the one seeking to dethrone God by both opposing Him and claiming His throne of rulership. But down through history he has had many agents, some of whom are in evidence in 2 Thessalonians 2. We will return to the identity of some of them in our next two chapters. Meanwhile, we need to examine the rest of the characteristics of the "man of lawlessness."

A fourth characteristic is that he is "the son of destruction" (verse 3). The term "destruction" can mean either one who causes destruction or one who experiences destruction. Here it undoubtedly applies to both the destructive activity of the lawless one and to his final destruction (pictured in verse 8) when Jesus returns again. We should note that the only other person to be labeled a "son of destruction" in all of Scripture is Judas (John 17:12). The fifth characteristic of the "man of lawlessness" is that he will most fully come in the future (after the removal of the restraint against him) "with all power and signs and false wonders" (2 Thess. 2:9). The next two chapters of this commentary will return to these five characteristics as they explore the identity of the "man of lawlessness" through the lenses of the Bible's overall teaching on apocalyptic and Christian history.

Verses 6 and 7 turn from the "man of lawlessness" to the one who holds him back until the time when he is permitted to expose or reveal the depth of his antichristian principles (verse 6b). Here the passage takes a definite turn to the future. The restraining occurs throughout Christian history. But when the full restraint is removed just before the coming of Christ, two things will transpire. First, (1) "the lawless one will be revealed" fully, and (2) the Lord Jesus returns and will destroy him "by the breath of His mouth" (verse 8). At that point Satan's schemes collapse along with those of his agents and followers.

The identity of the restrainer has created a great deal of discussion. Revelation 7:1 supplies the best answer with its snapshot of four angels of God holding back the destructive winds of strife right before the end of the world. When that restraint is gone, earth rushes into the final phases of human history, climaxed by the Second Advent (Rev. 19).

5. More Instruction Regarding the Great Apostasy

2 Thessalonians 2:8-12

[8]And then the lawless one will be revealed, whom the Lord will destroy by the breath of His mouth and will bring to an end by the appearance of His coming. [9]The coming [of the lawless one] will be according to the working of Satan, with all power and signs and false wonders, [10]and with every de-

ception of wickedness for those who are destroyed, because they did not accept the love of the truth that they might be saved. ¹¹God therefore sends them a powerful delusion so that they will believe the falsehood, ¹²in order that all those not believing the truth but having had pleasure in wrongdoing may be condemned.

"And then" are important words in the flow of 2 Thessalonians 2:1-12. Verses 3 and 4 described the historic lawless one who had already begun to operate in Paul's time (verse 7a) but whom God kept under control until it was time for him to be fully manifested (verse 6). However, the restraint would come to an end (verse 7). "And then" Paul "turns to what will happen exclusively in the future in 2:8-12." Then "the antichrist will make his long-awaited appearance on the scene of history in order to deceive the church on a massive scale." G. K. Beale asserts that "God is the one who ultimately holds back the antichrist from appearing (2:6-7), so that when he finally appears it is only because God has decided that it is 'the proper time' (2:7) to judge him and bring history to an end" (Beale, *1-2 Thessalonians,* p. 221). And it is at the end of history that Jesus will destroy the lawless one by "the breath of His mouth" (verse 8). Destruction by "breath" is another way of saying that it will be no difficult thing to do, that He won't even have to lift a hand.

Thus the import of the "and then" of verse 8 is that the text is shifting from the part the lawless one plays down through history to his future and final role at the end of time. Central to his activity at the end of time will be "the coming" of the lawless one "according to the working of Satan, with all power and signs and false wonders, and with every deception of wickedness" (verses 9, 10).

Of special importance in determining what Paul is talking about is the word "coming" (*parousia*) in verse 9. *Parousia* is the same word used repeatedly in the New Testament to describe the second coming of Jesus (see verses 1, 8; 1 Thess. 4:15). Beyond that, just as Christ returns in power and glory (2 Thess. 1:7, 8), so the lawless one will appear with power, signs, and wonders (2 Thess. 2:9). Scripture uses all three of those words of the miracles of Christ (see, e.g., Acts 2:22). What we have in verse 9 is a counterfeit of Jesus' second advent. John Stott suggests that Paul is describing "the coming of the Antichrist as a deliberate and unscrupulous parody of the second coming of Christ" (Stott, p. 172).

The apostle moves on in 2 Thessalonians 2:10 to emphasize the deceptiveness of the counterfeit. Jesus Himself referred to the power of that deception when He told His disciples, "If any one says to you, 'Lo, here is the Christ!' or 'There he is!' do not believe it. For false Christs and false prophets will arise and show great signs and wonders, so as to lead astray, if possible, even the elect" (Matt. 24:23, 24, RSV).

One student of the topic graphically pictures the event: "As the crowning act in the great drama of deception, Satan himself will personate Christ. The church has long professed to look to the Saviour's advent as the consummation of her hopes. Now the great deceiver will make it appear that Christ has come. In different parts of the earth, Satan will manifest himself among men as a majestic being of dazzling brightness, resembling the description of the Son of God given by John in the Revelation. Revelation 1:13-15. The glory that surrounds him is unsurpassed by anything that mortal eyes have yet beheld. The shout of triumph rings out upon the air: 'Christ has come! Christ has come!' The people prostrate themselves in adoration before him, while he lifts up his hands and pronounces a blessing upon them, as Christ blessed His disciples when He was upon the earth" (White, *The Great Controversy*, p. 624).

Paul does not hesitate to depict the false *parousia* as being accompanied by "every deception of wickedness" or "evil's undiluted power to

The Genuine *Parousia*

1. Jesus will descend from heaven (1 Thess. 4:16).
2. "Every eye shall see him" (Rev. 1:7, KJV).
3. It will be as visible as the lightning that flashes from the east to the west (Matt. 24:27).
4. A retinue of mighty angels and a trumpet blast will accompany Him (2 Thess. 1:7; 1 Thess. 4:16).
5. The righteous dead will be resurrected and meet Him in the air (1 Thess. 4:16).
6. Living believers will be caught up from the earth to meet Jesus and their resurrected friends (1 Thess. 4:17).

Satan may be able to counterfeit some things, but many of these events are beyond even his abilities. Thus no student of the Bible need be misled by the false *parousia*.

deceive" (2 Thess. 2:10, Phillips). Perhaps that is one reason why the New Testament seems to go out of its way to describe the true *parousia* of Christ. God doesn't want His sincere followers to be deceived. Because of the nature of some of the events that take place at the genuine return of Christ, it is impossible for Satan to counterfeit completely the Second Advent.

The second half of 2 Thessalonians 2:10 shifts the scene from the lawless one to his followers. Having said that they will be destroyed in the first part of the verse, the second offers the all-important information on *why* they will perish: "Because they did not accept the love of the truth that they might be saved." The truth in question is the gospel message that Paul had been teaching his followers. But please note that the apostle is not merely stating that they refused to accept the truth in cold doctrinal terms but that they had rejected "the *love* of the truth." Genuine biblical truth is never a theoretical abstraction. It always involves the whole person rather than only the mind. When Jesus said "I am . . . the truth" (John 14:6) He highlighted the fact that loving Christian truth means coming into a relationship with the God of that truth. The problem that Paul is speaking to in verse 10 is that some had rejected "the love of the truth." Thus even members of the church who have accepted true doctrines mentally may find themselves on the wrong side at the end of time because their religion was merely intellectual rather than something that has captured their hearts and lives.

Before we move away from the issue of truth we need to reflect upon the problem that many postmoderns and others have with the very concept of truth itself in the twenty-first century. Because in our age many view truth as relative and personal, we need a refresher course on the biblical perspective on truth. The apostle Paul was quite certain that some would be lost because they did not have a right relationship with truth. Jesus was just as firm when He claimed that He was *the* truth, *the* way, and *the* life (John 14:6). And Acts 4:12 asserts that "there is salvation in no one else, for there is no other name under heaven . . . by which we must be saved" (RSV). Apparently all religions do not lead to the same place. For Paul truth was not a take it or leave it matter. He was dead serious when he wrote that some would be deceived and lost eternally because "they refused to love the truth and so be saved" (2 Thess. 2:10, RSV).

Beale points out that verse 11 represents a "theological problem."

After all, "how can God be good and just and still *send them a powerful delusion so that they will believe the lie"?* (Beale, *1-2 Thessalonians*, p. 222). The answer is that "Paul writes as a Jew who ascribed all that happened to the direct personal action of God" (Bicknell, p. 78) or, alternately, "in the Scriptures God is often said to do that which He does not prevent" (Nichol, vol. 7, p. 274). Thus in Romans 1 Paul repeatedly declares regarding those who had rejected God and His values, that "God gave them up" to sin and its disastrous results (see verses 24, 26, 28). The Lord forces no one to follow Him. He lets people make their own choices and live by them, even if such decisions lead to believing "the falsehood" that results in their eventual condemnation (2 Thess. 2:11, 12).

In closing, we should note that the opposite of "believing the truth" in verse 12 is having "pleasure in wrongdoing" or "wickedness" (NIV). Truth has moral implications. Evil in the heart rather than mere error or ignorance is at the center of the problem highlighted by Paul. And that love of wrongdoing is the cause of people's ultimate condemnation (verse 12) and "eternal destruction" (2 Thess. 1:9).

Leon Morris perceptively sums up Paul's teaching: "The stark contrast reminds us that ultimately we must belong to one or other of two classes, namely, those who welcome and love God's truth and those who take their pleasure in wickedness. Those who begin by failing to accept God's good gift end up by setting forward unrighteousness. Notice the way in which they become perverted. These people are not described as sinning through force of circumstances or any form of compulsion. They now find their pleasure in sin. They delight in wrong. For them evil has become good" (Morris, *First and Second*, 1991, p. 236).

6. The Great Apostasy in Broader Perspective

Endless speculation has surrounded the nature of the apostasy and the identity of the lawless one of 2 Thessalonians 2:3-12. D. Edmond Hiebert makes an interesting statement on that passage when he asserts that "no other portion of the prophetic Scriptures covers precisely the same points of revelation here given" (Hiebert, p. 299).

His claim is interesting since, contrary to its assertion, the themes of prophetic scripture highlighted in 2 Thessalonians 2:3-9 are the dominant ones in New Testament apocalyptic even though they may not make "precisely the same points." Casting the word "precisely" aside, I would like to suggest that other parts of prophetic scripture in both testaments do make all of the same points.

We find the key to understanding New Testament apocalyptic in Matthew 24:15, in which Jesus refers readers back to the book of Daniel when he discusses the "abomination of desolation." His particular focus had to do with imperial Rome desecrating the Jerusalem Temple (Luke 21:20) based on Daniel 9:27. But other references to the "abomination of desolation" definitely refer to post-imperial Rome and always have to do with disrupting the true worship of God in the Temple (Dan. 11:31; 12:11; 8:11-13). Like the man of sin and the apostasy in 2 Thessalonians 2, the abomination of desolation finds different modes of expression in different eras of world history. But its core identity centers on "a rival religious system that takes a position of avowed hostility to the worship of the true God centering in the services of the sanctuary, or Temple. . . . This substitute system of worship is abominable, or detestable, because it stands in implacable opposition to that of the true God" (Horn, p. 7). Apocalyptic prophecy has a definite connection between the "abomination of desolation" in Daniel, the "man of lawlessness" in Thessalonians, and the "antichrist" of John's letters.

Before we go any further, we need to look a little more carefully at the meaning of antichrist. A quick definition is that antichrist is anyone who is either against Christ or who takes the place of Christ or seeks to do both. The original antichrist was Satan. And it is Satan who lurks behind every other exhibition of the antichrist spirit throughout history. Thus the antichrist and the man of lawlessness are different names for the same entity. And just as there have been different historical expressions of the man of lawlessness so has it been with antichrist. John said that "many antichrists" had already manifested themselves in his day (1 John 2:18). In like manner, Paul tells us that the man of lawlessness had already begun his work in his own time (2 Thess. 2:7). But there will also be a climactic end-time revelation of this anti-God entity in which he will be fully revealed (verse 9).

As noted above, the key to understanding New Testament apocalyptic prophecy appears in Matthew 24:15, in which Jesus demonstrates that He was utilizing the prophetic outline found in Daniel in His own teaching on the topic. After demonstrating the significant parallels between Matthew 24 and the book of Daniel, Hans LaRondelle summarizes by writing that "the Olivet discourse presents Christ's commentary on Daniel's apocalyptic prophecies. Jesus made historical applications all of which center around His first or His second advents. He thereby gave Daniel's forecast a christological interpretation, as the key to unlock apocalyptic prophecy" (LaRondelle, *End-time Prophecies*, pp. 35, 57).

LaRondelle in his pathbreaking research on the unity of biblical apocalyptic then demonstrates how Paul in 2 Thessalonians and John in the book of Revelation both build upon Jesus' use of Daniel. G. K. Beale has come to similar conclusions, although his survey is not nearly as comprehensive as LaRondelle's. In terms of the man of lawlessness in 2 Thessalonians 2:3, Beale writes that "in 2:4, Paul develops the prophecy about the antichrist from Daniel 11" (Beale, *1-2 Thessalonians*, p. 206). And as for the book of Revelation, Beale concludes that the whole of chapter 13, which closely parallels the material in 2 Thessalonians 2:3, 4 in

> ## The Meaning of Antichrist
>
> A term used only by John in the New Testament (1 John 2:18, 22; 4:3; 2 John 7), antichrist is "formed from *anti*, 'against,' or 'instead of,' and *Christos*, 'Christ.' The word may therefore mean one who opposes Christ, or one who claims to take the place of Christ, or one who combines both these functions" (Nichol, vol. 7, p. 643).

its first 8 verses, "has been shaped according to a formative Daniel 7 influ-ence," which is "evident from a common theological pattern which is re-peated throughout both Daniel 7 and Revelation 13" (Beale, *Use of Daniel*, pp. 244, 245).

Here we find a lesson that most students of apocalyptic fail to utilize. LaRondelle emphasizes an important understanding when he writes that "to see the full biblical picture of the church age, we must study the prophecies of Daniel, Jesus, Paul, and John's Apocalypse together. They il-luminate each other because they describe the same epoch of salvation his-tory that ends in Jesus' coming with the glory of God and His angels" (LaRondelle, *Light*, p. 34).

With his mention of the ending of the "epoch of salvation history" at the Second Advent, LaRondelle points us to the fact that the chain of Bible prophecy set forth by Daniel starts in his own time and is not completed until the setting up of God's kingdom at the return of Jesus (see Daniel 2:31-35, 38, 44, 45). Daniel replicates that pattern in the prophecies of chapters 7, 8, and 10-12 of his book. With that fact in mind, it is signifi-cant that Daniel's parallel to the man of lawlessness in 2 Thessalonians is not found at the beginning of Christian history but after the fourth beast of Daniel 7:7, 19, which represented the Roman Empire (see Shea, pp. 132-142, 152 for a helpful treatment of this topic). It is the little horn en-tity that comes to power after the fall of imperial Rome in the fifth cen-tury and who speaks "words against the Most High . . . and shall think to change . . . the law" (Dan. 7:25, RSV) that represents the prototype for Paul's man of lawlessness who "opposes and exalts himself above every so-called god" (2 Thess. 2:4). Thus, according to the time frame set forth by Daniel, the lawless one might have begun his activity in Paul's day (verse 7), but would come to special prominence after the demise of imperial Rome (Dan. 7:7, 8, 19, 20, 23, 24), and will not reach its climactic phase until the relaxing of the restraining right before the Advent of Christ (2 Thess. 2:7-9). At that time God will bring the ultimate lawless one and all his understudies to an end (verse 8; Dan. 7:26).

I have developed two tables to help in understanding more fully the unity of apocalyptic prophecy that runs throughout the Bible. The first table illustrates the close relationship between Christ's end-time teaching in Matthew 24 and that of Paul in his two letters to Thessalonica. The sec-

TABLE I
Parallels Between Matthew 24
and Thessalonians

Matthew 24	*Thessalonians*
Begins with advice not to be led astray on the timing of the Advent (24:4)	Presentation in 2 Thessalonians begins with advice on not being deceived on the timing of the Advent (2 Thess. 2:3)
Highlights Daniel's "Son of man" (Dan. 7:13) coming in the clouds of heaven (24:30, cf., Rev. 14:14)	Features Christ coming in the clouds (1 Thess. 4:15-17)
Warns against false christs (24:24)	Predicts an imitation of the Second Advent by the lawless one (2 Thess. 2:9)
The deceptive false christ will come with signs and wonders (24:24)	The evil one will utilize signs and wonders in his end-time deception (2 Thess. 2:9)
The Advent compared to the coming of a thief in the night (24:43)	The Lord will come like a thief in the night (1 Thess. 5:2)

TABLE II
Prophecy Parallels Between 2 Thessalonians and Daniel and Revelation

Daniel	2 Thessalonians	Revelation
Little horn puts himself above God's law by attempting to change it (7:25)	The lawless one (2:3)	Wars against those who keep God's law (12:17)
Speaks words against the Most High (7:25) and will magnify himself above God (11:36, 37)	Sets himself up as God (2:4)	Blasphemes God and utters haughty words (13:5, 6)
Makes war on the saints (7:21, 25)	Son of destruction (2:3)	Makes war on the saints (13:17)
———	Empowered by Satan (2:9)	Empowered by the dragon (13:2) who is Satan (12:9)
Tramples temple of God (8:11-13) and perverts true worship (11:31)	Takes over temple of God (2:4)	Blasphemes God's tabernacle (13:6)
Destroyed at end (7:26), but not by human power (8:25)	Destroyed by Jesus at Second Advent (2:3, 8)	Destroyed by Jesus at end of time (19; 20:10)

ond table indicates the parallel teaching on apocalyptic that starts with Daniel and runs through 2 Thessalonians 2 and the book of Revelation.

We have spent considerable time examining the unity of biblical apocalyptic as it repeatedly refers to the lawless one under various rubrics. Now we need to survey church history as to his identity.

Even though Irenaeus in about A.D. 180 identified the various guises of the lawless one presented in Matthew, Daniel, 2 Thessalonians, and 1 John as a religious figure who would act "as if he were Christ" (Irenaeus, *Against Heresies* 25.4), the normal view in the early church was to see imperial Rome in that role. That was quite understandable, given the emperors' claim to divinity and their repression and persecution of the church.

But, notes F. F. Bruce, "Christian perspective on the subject was naturally changed when the empire began to show favor to the church instead of persecuting it" (Bruce, p. 183). During the medieval period some, both from within and outside of the Roman Catholic Church, began to accuse a worldly papacy of behaving like the predicted lawless one (see Froom, vol. 1, pp. 796-806; vol. 2, pp. 21-31, 44-65, 142-158). That trend came to full bloom with Martin Luther, the Catholic priest who initiated the Protestant Reformation. Luther saw the papacy as the antichrist since it placed itself above God's word and therefore above God. "The pope," he asserted, "is the real antichrist who has raised himself over and set himself against Christ, for the pope will not permit Christians to be saved except by his own power" (Luther in Althaus, p. 421).

John Calvin, of the same mind, wrote that "Paul . . . does not speak of one individual, but of a kingdom, that was to be taken possession of by Satan, that he might set up a seat of abomination in the midst of God's temple—which we see accomplished in Popery" (Calvin, *Thessalonians*, p. 327). "Since," Calvin stated in his *Institutes*, "it is clear that the Roman pontiff has shamelessly transferred to himself what belonged to God alone and especially to Christ, we should have no doubt that he is the leader and standard-bearer of that impious and hateful kingdom" (Calvin, *Institutes* 4. 7. 25).

Part of the Roman Catholic reaction to the Reformation was to locate the prophecy of the antichrist at some point in history at which it could not be applied to the Roman church. Thus the Spanish Jesuit Alcazar in

1614 introduced the preterist scheme of prophetic interpretation, which shifted the fulfillment of the prophecies back to the early Roman emperors. Alternately, the Spanish Jesuit Ribera in 1580 set forth the antichrist as a future supernatural individual who would rebuild the Temple in Jerusalem and rule for three and one half years (see Froom, vol. 2, 484-505; LaRondelle, "Historicist Method," p. 85).

Many of the post-Reformation creeds, meanwhile, wrote their understanding of the lawless one into their basic statements of belief. Thus the Westminster Confession of Faith in 1647 proclaimed that "there is no other head of the Church but the Lord Jesus Christ: nor can the Pope of Rome, in any sense be head thereof; but is that Antichrist, that man of sin and son of perdition, that exalteth himself in the Church against Christ, and all that is called God" (Schaff, pp. 658, 659; cf. pp. 481, 484, 723, 739).

That interpretation predominated among Protestants up to the latter part of the nineteenth century. Thus such influential eighteenth- and nineteenth-century commentators as Adam Clark (vol. 6, pp. 568-570), Matthew Henry (vol. 6, p. 643), and Jamieson, Fausset, and Brown (vol. 3, part 3, pp. 473, 474) all feature the papacy as the lawless one.

That general unity in interpretation would deteriorate in the late nineteenth and early twentieth centuries as interpreters began to abandon the historicist perspective that views apocalyptic prophecy as beginning at the time of the prophet and continuing until the end of time, a view clearly set forth in such places as Daniel 2, 7, 8, 9, 11, 12 and in the book of Revelation (see especially chapter 12). The late twentieth century would find the liberal wing of Protestantism, having largely given up belief in predictive prophecy, identifying the man of sin with the emperor worship cult of Rome. On the other hand, those in the conservative dispensational wing shifted the fulfillment of the lawless one to the future, in line with the presentation of Ribera, when the antichrist will cause trouble for Christians from his seat of authority in the rebuilt Jerusalem. Those holding to the historicist view set forth in Daniel and Revelation, however, continue to see the papal power as the primary historical lawless one, although, in line with earlier interpreters, they hold that "antichristian tendencies produce different Antichrists" who "shall hereafter find their consummation in an individual exceeding them all in intensity of evil" (Jamieson, vol. 3, part 3, p. 474).

That consummative antichrist, of course, is Satan, who is both the original antichrist (Isa. 14:12-14; Eze. 28:2, 13-15) and the one who will imitate Christ's *parousia* or coming when God releases His restraint of him near the end of earthly history. At that time he meets his end (2 Thess. 2:8).

I have spent three chapters on the issues surrounding the lawless one because each of the major apocalyptic prophecies in the Bible features him at the very center. That being so, here is a topic we need to study and seek to understand, even if we never fully grasp it until Christ returns and we see more fully from the perspective of eternity the interaction of good and evil in world history. For that reason we can heartily agree with LaRondelle that "it is not sufficient to know the antichrist of the past. We need to arm ourselves with a correct understanding of the prophetic word of God for our time and for the end of the age. Enlightened by this knowledge, we will no longer be ignorant of Satan's schemes (2 Cor. 2:11)" (LaRondelle, *Light*, p. 35).

7. Instruction Regarding Holding On

2 Thessalonians 2:13–17

[13]*But we should always thank God concerning you, brothers beloved by the Lord, because God chose you from the beginning for salvation through sanctification by the Spirit and belief in the truth.* [14]*To this He called you through our gospel, that you might possess the glory of our Lord Jesus Christ.* [15]*So then, brothers, stand firm and hold to the traditions which you were taught, either by our words or by a letter from us.*

[16]*Now may our Lord Jesus Christ Himself and God our Father, who loved us and has given us eternal comfort and good hope through grace,* [17]*comfort your hearts and establish you in every good work and word.*

In difficult times people will naturally hold on to something. It is a natural reaction. You don't have to tell people in a speeding bus that suddenly brakes to grab something. Their reflexes have already passed on the order. Of course, they may have reached for the wrong thing and will still meet what could have been an avoidable disaster.

Twice in 2 Thessalonians 2:13-17 Paul refers to the stability of his flock in Thessalonica. But in that passage he divides the responsibility between the church members and the first two persons of the Trinity. Thus in verse 15 the apostle appeals to the church members to "stand firm and hold," while in verses 16 and 17 he prays that the Father and the Son would establish them. The one commonality between the two references is the "good word," those things taught them by Paul and his evangelistic colleagues through either their oral or written words. To Paul the good word and the apostolic teachings were important to hold on to as the church continued to be shaken by the traumatic events (such as social rejection and persecution) that it was already experiencing, but even more so by the climactic exposure of the lawless one that would come in the future. Not merely holding on but clinging to the correct support is at the heart of his counsel in verses 13-17.

The same Satan who had hindered Paul from returning to strengthen the Thessalonian believers (1 Thess. 2:18) also wanted to shake the new believers right out of the faith. Thus the apostle's concern that they stand firm in 1 Thessalonians 3:8 and that they not let false reports disturb them in 2 Thessalonians 2:2.

> Satan seeks to shake up and shake out believers in every area of their lives. He attacks Christians
> 1. physically,
> 2. socially,
> 3. economically,
> 4. intellectually, and
> 5. morally.
> A believer's only hope is to hold on to the God of grace and His Word.

The devil had attempted to weaken those new believers in nearly every aspect of their lives. On the physical front they had suffered persecution (1 Thess. 1:4-6; 3:2-4). It had led to rejection in their social lives and deprivation in their economic well-being. The assault also had intellectual implications through false teachings (2 Thess. 2:2, 3), and a moral side in Satan's attempt to get them to return to the licentious ways of the pagan lifestyle (1 Thess. 4:1-8). The devil left no stones unturned as he sought to get them to let go. He continues in our day to unnerve believers and to shake them out of their faith.

In the face of Satan's forceful attacks, Paul counsels believers to hold on to the God of grace who has saved them (2 Thess. 2:13-15) and can establish them (verse 17), and to God's good Word through which He instructs them in His comforting promises and the way of life (verses 15, 17).

In the process of telling them to cling to God, Paul presents us with what James Denney calls "a system of theology in miniature" (Denney, p. 342). It features several aspects. The first relates to the Godhead. Paul features all three members of the Trinity in his counsel to hold on in verses 13-17. First is the Holy Spirit who sanctifies or sets Christians apart for holy purposes (verse 13). Then come Jesus Christ and God the Father, who provide "eternal comfort and good hope through grace" (verse 16). We should note two things about the Godhead in verses 16 and 17. One is that the apostle places the Son before the Father in verse 16 (contrary to 1 Thess. 3:11) thereby implying their equality. A second is that even though Paul presents them as two persons, he utilizes singular participles to represent their activities. That "singular number represents Paul's conception of the two persons as one God" (Thomas, p. 477). Thus all three members of the Godhead are involved in human salvation.

That salvation itself forms a second aspect of this "system of theology in miniature." In a sequence quite similar to that found in Romans 8:29, 30, 2 Thessalonians 2:13, 14 sets forth the plan of salvation rooted in God's initiative. First, God *chose* fallen sinners for salvation. But He didn't leave it up to them to find their own way out of their lostness. To the contrary, He *called* them through gospel preaching. That led to their *belief* in the truth and their being *set apart* or sanctified by the Holy Spirit in order that they might "possess the glory of our Lord Jesus Christ."

Here we need to stop and explore the concept of participating in Christ's glory, a topic that most of us modern Christians don't think much about. But both Paul (Rom. 8:30) and Peter (1 Peter 5:10) emphasize the fact that believers have been called to share God's eternal glory and to be glorified in Him. The promise of receiving glory is one of the great hopes of Christianity (see 1 Thess. 2:12; Rom. 5:2; 8:17; Col. 1:27). Given the fact that the Christians in Thessalonica were being dishonored in their community, the reality of future honor and meaning was especially meaningful. That glory was all the more important to the Thessalonian believers since, as Bruce Malina points out, "honor and shame" were central concerns in the first-century Mediterranean world (Malina, pp. 27-57).

Of course, if we who live in the twenty-first century examine our hearts we will discover that things haven't changed all that much. The fear of public shame and the joy of public honor still form an important aspect of our psychosocial selves. It is no accident that the New Testament repeatedly emphasizes the future glorification of God's people who have given their lives for Him on this earth. The promise of sharing Christ's glory has provided hope to Christians and encouraged them to hold on across history, and it continues to do so today.

Second Thessalonians 2:15 presents a crucial aspect of maintaining faith when Paul tells the Thessalonians to "stand firm and hold to the traditions which you were taught, either by our words or by a letter from us." One of the great anchors of faith throughout the apostolic writings is the words of Jesus and the New Testament writers. In 2 Thessalonians 2:15 the traditions *(paradoseis)* are not those of the church but the words of Paul based on what he had personally taught the Thessalonians in his previous letter to them and in his evangelism among them, which he has repeatedly pointed them back to (1 Thess. 2:13; 4:1, 2; 2 Thess. 2:5; 3:6). Of course, the current letter would now join that collection of information. Jude was of the same mind when he appealed to his readers "to contend for the faith which was once for all delivered to the saints" (Jude 3, RSV). And John echoed the same thought when he repeatedly referred his followers back to the apostolic word they had heard from "the beginning" (1 John 2:7, 24; 3:11; 2 John 6).

Paul had no doubt that what he had taught them during his initial evangelistic mission to them was the Word of God (1 Thess. 2:13). Along that line is Peter's teaching that even in his day believers considered Paul's writings to be scripture (2 Peter 3:16). And Paul himself reflects the apostolic consensus when he writes of the "sacred writings which are able to instruct you for salvation through faith in Christ Jesus" (2 Tim. 3:15, RSV). While that verse probably refers primarily to the Old Testament, it in no way excludes the apostolic writings, which were, by the time of Paul's letters to Timothy, also being viewed as scriptural. The apostolic teachings (along with the Old Testament) formed the basis for Christian faith in the earliest Christian communities. And the New Testament writers are consistent in citing that teaching as the authoritative test for all future understandings. Reflecting upon 2 Thessalonians 2:15, Victor Paul

Furnish notes that "the writer appears to reject in principle any notion that the apostolic tradition is open to changes" (Furnish, p. 168). It is that tradition that provides believers with what they need to know as they hold on in the face of life's trials and the devil's attacks.

Paul's passage on holding on includes a thanksgiving for their faith up to that point (2 Thess. 2:13, 14), an appeal to them to continue to hold on in the future (verse 15), and a prayer for God to comfort and establish them (verses 16, 17). Featured in that prayer is the fact that Christian hope and comfort and the power to hold on are founded on the love and grace of God. But that grace does not do it all. It is a combined endeavor as the God of grace enables His followers to continue in faith. It is a shared responsibility. Even as God supplies salvation through His love and grace, believers must daily decide to cling to the source of that power as set forth in the apostolic tradition—or to let go. Thus the appeal to them to "stand firm" and to "hold to the traditions" they were taught (verse 15). If they do so, God will do His part in establishing them "in every good work and word" (verse 17). But in the long run it is God's love and grace that lies at the foundation of all Christian hope, comfort, and stability. After all, "our stability is not only impossible, but actually inconceivable, apart from the steadfastness of the love of God" (Stott, p. 180).

Part III

Exhortations

2 Thessalonians 3:1-15

8. Exhortation to Pray

2 Thessalonians 3:1-5

> ¹*Finally, brothers, pray for us, that the word of the Lord will advance rapidly and be glorified, even as it did also with you, ²and that we will be delivered from wicked and evil men; for not all have faith. ³But faithful is the Lord, who will strengthen you and protect you from the evil one. ⁴And we have confidence in the Lord concerning you, that you are doing and will continue to do what things we command. ⁵Now may the Lord direct your hearts into the love of God and into the perseverance of Christ.*

Paul was a great man. But that greatness "consisted not so much in sheer native ability (though he had his share of that) as in his recognition of his dependence upon God" (Morris, *First and Second,* 1991, p. 245). That realization led him repeatedly to request that his converts pray for him and his ministry. The apostle knew where his power came from. Thus he did not place himself above those he had led to Christ. To the contrary, in his repeated requests for their prayers, he indicated that he was one with them in the struggles of life.

Near the end of 1 Thessalonians he had also solicited their prayers on his and his fellow laborers' behalf (1 Thess. 5:25), but there the request was general. Here in 2 Thessalonians it is specific. The first thing he asks them to pray for is that "the word of the Lord will advance rapidly" (2 Thess. 3:1). The word translated "advance rapidly" literally means "to run."

The apostle had in the past seen the gospel message run rapidly and spread at great speed. It had been so in Thessalonica itself, where in a few short weeks it had taken root quickly and deeply. But since leaving that vibrant congregation Paul had had more difficult times in such places as Athens. There it hardly advanced at all.

N. T. Wright likens Paul's experience in Athens to a frustrating dream that many of us have experienced. In it we need to run, but find that it is impossible. With legs feeling like lead and hopelessly heavy, we struggle but can hardly move them. Paul had gone through that kind of agony in some of his evangelistic work. But he longed that the gospel "word might 'run,' that is, that it might make its way freely into people's hearts and lives, changing them and forming them into a holy and loving people who would bring God glory in the world" (Wright, p. 153).

He knew that prayer was the only thing that could remove the hidden chains holding back the spread of the gospel message. Thus his request. But here we have a forceful lesson needed by the modern church. Namely, that God's leaders on earth require *our* prayers. They may be "great" preachers or evangelists, but that greatness is not intrinsically theirs. It is a gift from that God who not only gives talents but energizes their use through the power of the Holy Spirit. Only eternity will reveal the massive contribution made by the prayers of the unknown and unheralded people in the pews who pray earnestly and perseveringly for the progress of the gospel.

The image of the gospel word "running" is rooted in Psalm 147:15 in which God "sends forth his command to the earth; his word runs swiftly" (RSV). But while that is true, Paul undoubtedly also had the Greek games in mind. He repeatedly used running a race as a metaphor for the apostolic mission (1 Cor. 9:24-26; Gal. 2:2; Phil. 2:16).

In line with the Greek games image of running is the apostle's use of "glorified" in verse 1. After all, it is the successful runner who is crowned and honored in a race. And from Paul's perspective the gospel message could use a dose of honor. Not far from his mind was the brutal fact that he and his message had been run out of Philippi, Thessalonica, and Berea in rapid succession and ignored in Athens. In that light it is not difficult to see why the apostle not only asked that they pray for the rapid spread of the gospel word but also for its honor.

In verse 2 he adds a second request for their prayers—that "we will be delivered from wicked and evil men." George Milligan points out that both of the adjectives used of those men reflect "not so much of passive badness as of active harmfulness" (Milligan, p. 110). That had certainly been so in Paul's case. "Five times," he notes in another connection, "I have received at the hands of the Jews the forty lashes less one. Three times I have been beaten with rods; once I was stoned." And then there also existed "dangers" from Gentiles and from "false brethren" (2 Cor. 11:24-26, RSV).

While Paul could have been referring to any of several categories of "wicked and evil men" in 2 Thessalonians 3:2, he probably has fanatical Jews in mind. It had been that group that had stirred up the problems that forced him out of Thessalonica and Berea (Acts 17:5, 13) and that was currently causing him difficulties in Corinth (Acts 18:12-17), from which he wrote his letters to the Thessalonians.

At the root of the problem of the "wicked and evil men" was their lack of faith. They were not only actively against Paul, but were faithless (2 Thess. 3:2). But, he highlights in verse 3 in a play on words, God is "faithful." And in His faithfulness He strengthens and protects.

With that affirmation the apostle presents us with an important pastoral surprise. He had been relating his own difficulties and need of prayer in the face of evil people, but when he speaks of God's faithfulness he unexpectedly shifts the focus from himself to the Thessalonian believers who were also suffering from the same sort of "wicked and evil men." Thus he tells them that their faithful God "will strengthen you and protect you from the evil one" (verse 3). Here is a lesson of the highest magnitude in Paul's understanding of pastoral leadership. Even though all of them were suffering, with probably none of them undergoing as much intense and extended persecution as himself, yet his pastoral concern for his flock lifts him above personal considerations as he expresses his firm belief that God will strengthen and protect them. Herein the apostle's true Christian greatness again stands out. He was not only humble in asking for their prayers, but was selfless in his concern for those whom he had brought into the faith. Here we find Paul at his best as an example of what a Christian and a pastor should be.

With the use of the definite article in labeling their adversary as "*the* evil one" (verse 3) he again expresses his view that it was the quite personal Satan who was behind the "evil and wicked men" (see 1 Thess. 2:18). That understanding is consistent with Ephesians 6:12, in which he notes that Christians "are not contending against flesh and blood, but against the principalities, against the powers, against the world rulers of this

193

present darkness, against the spiritual hosts of wickedness in the heavenly places" (RSV). In Ephesians 2:2 Paul labels "the evil one" at the root of the problem as "the prince of the power of the air" (RSV) and in 2 Thessalonians he has already referred to him as the ultimate lawless one who is behind all of the other lawless ones (2 Thess. 2:3).

The apostle Paul had no doubt about the reality of the devil and his designs. On the other hand, many modern sophisticates have no such understanding. Evil for them is merely an impersonal force that we can conquer through social reform. But Martin Luther had the only adequate answer for such people. "If you don't believe in the devil," he asserted, "it's because you've never resisted him" (cited in Demarest, p. 134). All too many in Luther's day and ours lack the apostle's understanding of "the evil one" (2 Thess. 2:3) behind all the "wicked and evil men" (verse 2). As a result, they are marching to his tune whether they believe in him or not. Such is the deception of the spiritual warfare that was so real in Paul's life.

The concept of faith has an interesting journey in 2 Thessalonians 3:2-4. Verse 2 speaks of those who lack faith, verse 3 turns to the faithfulness of God, and verse 4, even though it does not use the word, reflects on the living faith or faithfulness of the Thessalonian believers when Paul commends their life of faith in doing and continuing to do what he has commanded. While he has no doubt about their past faithfulness, his emphasis is probably on their future actions, a topic that he will counsel them on in verses 6-15.

In the meantime, the apostle closes off his exhortation on prayer by offering one for the Thessalonian believers themselves. He specifically prays that their hearts might be directed to God's love and "into the patient perseverance of Christ" (verse 5). I have translated *hupomonēn* as "perseverance" rather than the equally acceptable "endurance" because Paul and the rest of the New Testament authors present the Christian life more in terms of the activity implied in "perseverance" than the passivity inherent in "endurance." In short "endurance" is what people experience when something is happening to them, while "perseverance" emphasizes something that people do. While both words reflect Christian experience, it seems to me that "perseverance" most accurately expresses the outgoing faith of the running or rapidly advancing word that Paul spoke of in verse 1 and that is seen in the ministry of Christ, who provides the believer's model in verse 5.

9. Exhortation to Work

2 Thessalonians 3:6-13

⁶Now, brothers, we command you in the name of our Lord Jesus Christ, that you keep away from every brother who lives irresponsibly and not according to the tradition which you received from us. ⁷For you yourselves know how you ought to imitate us, because we were not disorderly among you, ⁸nor did we eat anyone's bread without paying, but in toil and hardship we worked night and day so that we would not be a burden to any of you; ⁹not because we did not have the right, but that we ourselves might provide a pattern for you to imitate us. ¹⁰For even when we were with you, we commanded you this: that if anyone does not want to work, let him not eat either. ¹¹For we hear of some living among you who are irresponsible, not working at all, but being busybodies. ¹²Now such persons we command and exhort in the Lord Jesus Christ to work with quietness that they may eat their own bread. ¹³But you, brothers, do not be weary in doing good.

Sometimes people just don't listen to me! Have you ever felt that way? The sad news is that it is not only a problem with us ordinary mortals. The apostle Paul faced it also.

In his first letter he had specifically addressed the fact that some of the Thessalonian believers had given up work and were not minding their own business (1 Thess. 4:11). And that wasn't the first time he had had to face that problem among them. He had specifically "commanded" them to work when he first evangelized their community, forcefully telling them "that if anyone does not want to work, let him not eat either" (2 Thess. 3:10).

But some among the Thessalonians didn't listen to Paul then. Nor did they pay attention to his comments on the topic in his first letter, even though he raised the subject twice (1 Thess. 4:11; 5:14). As a result, he allots the bulk of chapter 3 (verses 6-15) in his second letter to this persistent problem in what was otherwise a model congregation. In fact, outside of the issue of the misunderstanding regarding the Second Advent (2 Thess. 2:1-12), the problem of nonworking members is 2 Thessalonians' dominant topic.

It is undoubtedly no accident that Paul places the problems of idleness and being busybodies (1 Thess. 4:11; 5:14; 2 Thess. 3:11) in both letters in the context of the second coming of Jesus (1 Thess. 4:13-5:11; 2 Thess.

2:1-11). It appears that in the emotional excitement of what they believed was the very imminent return of Christ, they had abandoned their daily work as they awaited that event. And, to make matters worse, instead of minding that needful business, they were busy agitating other people. Or, as Leon Morris puts it, "we may conjecture that they were trying to do one or both of two incompatible things, namely, to get their living from others, and to persuade those others to share their point of view about the second advent and so get them to stop working too" (Morris, *First and Second*, 1991, p. 257).

Five Stages in Handling a Persistent Problem

1. Paul expresses confidence in the church as a whole about doing what he has commanded (2 Thess. 3:4).
2. He commands the faithful members to keep away from the disorderly (verse 6).
3. He reminds them of the principle regarding work that he had taught them during his visit (verse 10).
4. He directly addresses the disorderly (verse 11).
5. He provides instructions for church discipline of those who might still ignore his teaching (verses 14, 15).

Having twice failed to make himself heard on this troublesome topic, Paul gives it major space in his second letter. In the process he speaks very plainly so that the Thessalonian believers cannot possibly fail to understand him. Beyond that, he concludes by telling the church that it needs to take redemptive discipline against those who do not heed him on the subject (2 Thess. 3:14, 15).

We find Paul at his pastoral best in dealing with a difficult congregational issue in 2 Thessalonians 3. On the one hand, he is positive in affirming the congregation of his confidence in them, while at the same time referring to those not following his instruction as "brothers" (verse 6).

But the apostle's brotherly love for the offenders is not a mushy type that merely accepts their misconduct. To the contrary, it is "tough love," a love that faces up to them and seeks to correct their ways. We see that tough love flashed forth in the thrice repeated word for their irresponsibility or disorderliness (verses 6, 7, 11). While the Revised Standard Version and the New International Version translate *atakteō* as "idleness," its actual meaning is "to be neglectful of duty" or "to lead a disorderly life." It is a military term used "of soldiers marching out of order" (Thayer, p. 83). "The specific manner in which the irresponsible behavior manifests itself is described in the context: freeloading, sponging" (Bauer, p. 148).

Paul confronts that irresponsible behavior with another word with military overtones. "We command," he asserts in verses 6, 10, and 12. He makes it clear that he is not providing good advice or merely making a request. No! He is ordering them in no uncertain terms to shape up and to get in step or to get into line.

Beyond that, Paul tells the congregation the consequences they will face for not following his orders:

1. First, those who continue to disobey are to be shunned by the rest of the congregation (verse 6). That was a serious issue in a community already rejected by the surrounding culture. If they were also ostracized by the Christian community, they would truly be alone. But that aloneness might, hopefully, wake them up. If not, further steps would be needed.

2. Second, cut off their food supply (verse 10). In short, starve them into opening their eyes to the facts of their disobedient situation. Here the apostle is not coddling weak saints who don't know what they are doing. Rather, he is in the business of shocking persistently rebellious sinners into responsible action.

3. But if that doesn't work, Paul has a third tactic in his arsenal to wake them up, one we will examine in our treatment of verses 14 and 15 in our next chapter.

The implication is clear in Paul's treatment of the topic. Not only do individuals have a responsibility in making certain that the church is marching according to the commands of God, but also the church itself. Here we have an issue that many congregations in our day do not want to hear. Unfortunately for that mind-set, Paul felt otherwise. As a result, we will follow him in highlighting the topic in our next chapter.

In the meantime, Paul resurrects a few themes from 1 Thessalonians related to the problem. The first of those is imitation. In 1 Thessalonians 1:6 Paul had commended the Thessalonians for being imitators of his apostolic team and of Jesus. And in the second chapter the apostle noted that the persecuted believers had emulated the churches in Judea in their sufferings (verse 14). In 2 Thessalonians he utilizes the imitation motif in the framework of following the apostolic team's orderly conduct in terms of laboring to support themselves (2 Thess. 3:7-9).

That thought led Paul to repeat the fact that he and his colleagues in ministry had labored "night and day" in "toil and hardship," phrases he had used earlier in 1 Thessalonians 2:9. In both cases Paul emphasizes that the reason for their hard labor was so that they might not burden the churches. But in 1 Thessalonians 2:9 he tied their hard labor to preaching the gospel to them, whereas in 2 Thessalonians he connects it to the fact that the troublemakers needed to reflect the orderly pattern that the apostolic team had set forth as they labored to provide for their own needs. The logic is clear. If busy apostles could labor for their keep, then the lazy busybodies who had no business except "minding everybody's business but their own" (2 Thess. 3:11, REB) had absolutely no excuse for not working to care for their own needs.

In addition, Paul reminds them that as ministers of the gospel, he and his colleagues had a "right" to receive support from their converts. He treats that "right" most thoroughly in 1 Corinthians 9:3-14. Verse 14 makes it plain that "the Lord commanded that those who proclaim the gospel should get their living by the gospel" (RSV). But Paul had worked in spite of the fact that he could have called upon his apostolic rights. The disorderly ones in Thessalonica had no such rights. Yet they were acting as if they did. Such individuals, Paul implies, were deluded and a blot on the church. They needed to wake up. And if they couldn't do that on their own with Paul's commands before them, then the church needed to take vigorous and unmistakable action. It is to that topic that we now turn.

But before doing so we need to reflect on Paul's last words in the paragraph running from 2 Thessalonians 3:6-13: "But you, brothers, do not be weary in doing good" (verse 13). The idea is that even though some people in the church are rebellious despite all that is being done to wake them up, we need to be patient in seeking to do good for them through our continued efforts for them. Here is a challenge for anyone who has ever tried to help someone determined to follow the wrong path.

10. Exhortation Regarding Church Discipline

2 Thessalonians 3:14, 15

[14]Now if anyone does not obey our instruction in this letter, make note of that person and do not associate with him, so that he may be put to shame. [15]Yet do not regard him as an enemy, but warn him as a brother.

In verse 14 we come face to face with a topic generally avoided in modern congregations. Firm church discipline is out of style in the twenty-first century. And in part for good reason. N. T. Wright points out that "much contemporary culture has reacted so strongly against the abuse of power, and then against the exercise of power or discipline in any sphere, that the mere suggestion of it conjures up images of people being burnt at the stake, or of the horrors of the Inquisition. We now have so embraced the idea of everyone being free to follow their own way that we recoil" from church discipline in any form (Wright, p. 159).

"Let's just be loving," is the cry of the modern, liberated church member in the face of a moral problem in the church. And by being loving they generally mean accepting and being quiet about the offense—acting as if it didn't exist. But such an approach finds no home in the New Testament. "The Lord," we read in Hebrews 12:6, "disciplines him whom he loves" (RSV). And even in the family context it is the parent who disciplines who demonstrates genuine love, rather than those who ignore the problem and let the child sail into a life of disaster. To love is to care enough to take the effort to correct the erring.

It is in that spirit of loving care that Paul sets forth some of the New Testament's most important instruction on church discipline. John Stott presents five helpful practical guidelines on church discipline that flow out of Paul's treatment of the topic in 2 Thessalonians 3:14, 15 (see Stott, pp. 193, 194). First, the *need* for discipline. Discipline is necessary when dealing with public defiance of apostolic instruction. Paul provided the counsel in verses 14 and 15 because he anticipated that some of the disorderly individuals of verses 6-13 would not fall into line, even with commands given "in the name of our Lord Jesus Christ" (verse 6). The apostle had warned the idlers at least three times. Yet they were apparently going to continue as if he had said nothing. Thus they demonstrated that they cared for neither the health of the Christian community nor for its reputation in the wider Thessalonian culture. As a result, Paul asserts in forceful terms that those who obstinately refused to obey must be disciplined (verse 14).

Second, the *nature* of discipline, which in this case was social ostracism. The apostle had introduced that topic in verse 6, in which he commanded the faithful members to "keep away from every brother who lives irresponsibly and not according to the tradition which you received from us."

In verse 14 the rightfully agitated apostle becomes even more explicit as he sets forth two steps in the disciplinary process. One is to "take note of" that person or "mark" or "put a tag" on him or her as a troublemaker (Rogers, p. 486). E. J. Bicknell suggests that such a marking might mean noting "the offender down in your own mind so as to keep aloof from him, or it may mean some form of public censure as by bringing his name before the gathering" of the church (Bicknell, p. 94). It probably in this case had the more public significance. That would especially be true since 2 Thessalonians would undoubtedly be read publicly before the entire congregation, as Paul had commanded regarding the first letter (1 Thess. 5:27). By the time of the public reading of 2 Thessalonians 3 everybody would know who the marked individuals were—those who absolutely refused to obey the apostolic word.

Another aspect of the discipline was the command to avoid those who continued to rebel. The words translated as "not associate" are used only one other time in the New Testament. First Corinthians 5:11 orders the faithful "not to associate with any one who bears the name of brother if he is guilty of immorality or greed, or is an idolater, reviler, drunkard, or robber" (RSV). But there the offense is more serious and the separation total. On the other hand, the Thessalonian command contains the moderating words "do not regard him as an enemy, but warn him as a brother." "Reformation, not exclusion from the brotherhood, is intended" in verses 14 and 15 (Frame, p. 309).

It is in line with that redemptive aim that Paul adds "so that he may be put to shame" (verse 14). David deSilva helps us see the forcefulness of such ostracism when he writes that "honor and dishonor represent the primary means of social control in the ancient Mediterranean world." As a result, "first-century Mediterranean people were oriented from early childhood to seek honor and avoid disgrace, meaning that they would be sensitive to public recognition or reproach" (deSilva in Evans, pp. 519, 518). In such a context, the combination of social shunning and the public reading of a document that identified or marked them would have a powerful impact and would hopefully lead them into harmony with both apostolic teaching and their congregation.

Beyond the need for discipline and its nature, 2 Thessalonians 3:14, 15 also highlights those *responsible* for its administration. As in verses 6-13, church discipline is the responsibility of the entire congregation. Paul is not merely addressing the elders who are "over" them (1 Thess. 5:12), but the entire body of the church. As Stott notes, "leaders may need to take the initiative, but then a corporate decision and corporate action should be taken by the whole church membership. Without this, rival factions are bound to develop" (Stott, p. 194).

> ## A Perspective on Church Discipline
>
> "Maybe the most significant thing we can learn from such a text is how far many of us are removed from a view of the church in which the dynamic of the Spirit was so real that exclusion could be a genuinely redemptive action" (Fee, *1 Corinthians*, p. 214).

A fourth element of church discipline is the *spirit* in which a congregation must administer it. Here Paul is quite explicit that the congregation must treat offenders as family members (brothers and sisters) rather than enemies (2 Thess. 3:15). He makes the same point in Galatians 6:1, in which he counsels that "if a man is overtaken in any trespass, you who are spiritual should restore him in a spirit of gentleness" (RSV).

The fifth aspect stressed is the *purpose* of church discipline. It is not out to destroy the wayward but to restore them to harmony with the body of the church. Jesus advocated the same principle when He noted that the correct treatment of a wrong doer can lead to gaining a brother or sister (Matt. 18:15).

Before leaving 2 Thessalonians 3:14, 15 we should note that perhaps a topic almost as much out of harmony with the postmodern mind as church discipline is that of apostolic authority. All too many, even in the churches, look to the Bible as merely good advice that they can either accept or reject in line with their predispositions or lifestyle. But Paul rejected such an approach. He knew that his teachings came with the full authority of the Lord Jesus behind them. And what was true of Paul held for the rest of the writers of the New Testament. They recognized that they were transmitting to the church for all time the authoritative Word of God. It was that all-important Word that was to form the foundation for belief and lifestyle in the Thessalonian church. Any church member who rejected that Word stood under condemnation. Postmodern Christians might not like such teachings. But like them or not, they stand as the basis of the Christian faith even in our day.

Part IV

Closing Matters

2 Thessalonians 3:16-18

11. Final Blessings

2 Thessalonians 3:16-18

[16]Now may the Lord of peace Himself give you peace continually in every way. The Lord be with you all.

[17]I, Paul, write this greeting with my own hand, which is a sign in every letter. It is the way I write. [18]The grace of our Lord Jesus Christ be with you all.

Paul's closing thoughts in verses 16 through 18 consist of two blessings or benedictions with a personal note of the letter's authenticity sandwiched in between them. It should not surprise us that "peace" and "grace" dominate the blessings. Both words were central to the apostle's understanding of the gospel and appear in the introductions to both of the Thessalonian letters (1 Thess. 1:1; 2 Thess. 1:2) and also their conclusions (1 Thess. 5:23, 28; 2 Thess. 3:16, 18).

Furthermore, it is no accident that the prayer/blessing of peace dominates the first benediction of 2 Thessalonians 3:16. The believers in Thessalonica needed nothing more than peace. In verse 15 Paul had just finished telling them not to deal with those causing disruption in their congregation as if they were enemies, indicating that in itself it required the peace he wishes for them. But even more problematic for the Thessalonian believers was that they had been facing tension, discrimination, and persecution from the surrounding secular community ever since Paul and his associates had founded their church (Acts 17:5; 1 Thess. 2:14).

Three points stand out in the first blessing. The first is that Paul directs his prayer to the "Lord of peace." Here we have a reference to the Old Testament "Prince of Peace," the Son who would usher in the messianic kingdom (Isa. 9:6, 7). We also find an echo of the words of Jesus near the end of His life when He bestowed upon His disciples the peace they needed so much in a time of crisis (John 14:27). And Paul himself had no doubts that Jesus "is our peace" (Eph. 2:14) and was thus uniquely qualified to provide peace to the Thessalonians, even in their stressful situation.

"Peace," we should note, means more than the absence of conflict. As we have pointed out before, its broader meaning in the Bible comes from the Hebrew *shalom*, a term meaning complete well-being. And Paul is clear that such a state of well-being comes through a person's being right with God through Jesus. Thus Christians have peace because they have been "justified by faith" (Rom. 5:1, RSV).

A second thing prominent in the blessing of 2 Thessalonians 3:16 is that the prayer is directed toward Jesus, "the Lord of peace Himself." That parallels the closing prayer of 1 Thessalonians 5:23, but with a major difference. In the first letter the prayer addresses God, while in the second Paul directs it to Jesus. Thus we find the easy-going, natural equation of Jesus as being equal with the Father that flows throughout the Thessalonian correspondence. The letters abound in Trinitarian assumptions and allusions from beginning to end (see the discussion of "Jesus is 'Lord'" under "Major Themes of 1 Thessalonians" in the introduction to that letter).

A third point to consider in the blessing of 2 Thessalonians 3:16 is the "all." The prayer is not merely for the faithful in the congregation. Rather, it is for them "all," the entire body of the church. Here is an important insight encapsulated in a small word. Church members who have made mistakes are still God's children. They are still part of the "all" of Paul's blessing. There may come occasions when church discipline—even disfellowshipping—is needed (1 Cor. 5:13), but until the time when their ongoing rebellion has run its course they are still brothers and sisters and are to be worked with rather than treated as enemies (2 Thess. 3:14, 15). Thus Paul's blessing is for the entire congregation, for each and every member, for "all" of them. In that inclusive approach the apostle was following the Lord of grace as he dealt with struggling members.

Tucked in between the blessings of verses 16 and 18 is the informative verse 17. Here Paul not only tells them that he is signing the letter with his own hand, but that his autograph is a sign for them. That he added a final greeting in his own handwriting is not unique to 2 Thessalonians. It is a feature that not only shows up in several of his other letters (1 Cor. 16:21; Gal. 6:11; Col. 4:18; Philemon 19), but one that was common in the correspondence of many others of that era. A secretary may have written the bulk of most letters, but the one dictating often signed off using his or her own name. What is unique about 2 Thessalonians 3:17 is that the apostle says that his signature is a "sign," by which he undoubtedly meant that it was an indication of the letter's authenticity or "proof that it really is from me" (TLB). That proof or sign was especially needed in Thessalonica since someone had apparently forged a letter claiming to be from Paul in order to add strength to a false understanding that he or she was seeking to convince the congregation of (see 2 Thess. 2:2). Paul wrote 2 Thessalonians, of course, to counteract that false theology. As a result, the apostle wanted them to be certain that this letter with its correct understanding was really from him.

Before leaving Paul's note on the letter's authenticity, we should consider two other points. First, Paul leaves no doubt that he, himself ("I, Paul"), is the primary author of the letter. Silvanus and Timothy may have been included in the greetings and may have been partners with Paul in his evangelism in Thessalonica and may have discussed with Paul the issues contained in it, but it was Paul who dictated the letter and signed off with his own distinctive and authoritative signature.

A second point is a general consensus among students of Paul that he probably signed all of his letters whether he mentioned that signing or not. That is probably the significance of "it is the way I write" at the end of 2 Thessalonians 3:17. But, given the problem of a false letter purporting to be from Paul in the Thessalonian community, he went out of his way in that letter not only to call attention to his signature but to the fact that his signature was a sign. Such a comment would not be needed for anyone reading the letter. They would see the change in handwriting from that of the secretary to that of the author (see Gal. 6:11), but that would not be recognized by those hearing a letter being read publicly to the assembled congregation, one way in which Paul communicated his teachings to the churches he corresponded with (see 1 Thess. 5:27).

Paul's final blessing centers on grace, the very word he begins his initial greetings with in both of his letters to Thessalonica (1 Thess. 1:1; 2 Thess. 1:2). How fitting! The grace of God through Jesus stands at the very heart of Paul's theology. God's free gift of grace is the source not only of salvation (Eph. 2:8), it is the root of that peace with God that he prayed for in the blessing of verse 16 (see Rom. 5:1).

The final blessing of 2 Thessalonians is exactly the same as that in the first letter (1 Thess. 5:28) with the exception of the added word "all" in 2 Thessalonians. Paul may have had some hard things to say to some of the Thessalonian believers, but he includes "all" of them in his final prayer. His pastoral heart yearned for their healing.

There is a wideness in God's mercy that His church needs to embrace even as it deals with difficult people. And "difficult people," in one way or another, includes "all" of us in the twenty-first-century church. "All" of us are on a journey into that full sanctification that Paul prayed for the Thessalonians in the conclusion to his first letter (1 Thess. 5:23). While some church members may be hung up on the more rebellious and open forms of sin, others in the church unconsciously exude the self-righteous attitude of the "Christian Pharisee." All of us need God's grace. All of us need God's peace. All of us are included in Paul's final "all." And for that we can all thank God.